Global Market Strategies

T0345925

E-Book inside

Please find the download directions to your free ebook at the end of this book.

Born in Germany in 1968 Michael Neubert studied at a number of internationally prestigious universities including Columbia Business School, the University of St. Gallen in Switzerland and the University of Bayreuth in Germany. He gained his doctorate in Business Administration. He has been working in international management for more than twenty years and this has taken him to almost every corner of the earth. His jobs have ranged from international project manager to head of a foreign department and from the managing director of an overseas branch office to the post of CEO of an international corporation.

Since 2006, Michael Neubert has been lecturing and conducting research in the field of international and intercultural management at various renowned universities. In 2011 Michael Neubert also founded the *C2NM company2newmarket LLC*, which supports organizations in developing new foreign markets and increasing their intercultural competence. Moreover, he is actively engaged in companies with high internationalization potential.

Michael Neubert speaks six languages and has lived in seven different countries. He has published a number of articles on the topic of 'International Management' and is very enthusiastic about the international environment in which he finds himself. He is particularly proud of his library with its comprehensive selection of books on the subject of 'International Management'. He is author of 'Internationale Markterschließung' (Developing International Markets) (3rd edition 2011 / MI Wirtschaftsbuch – Münchner Verlagsgruppe) and co-author of 'Wie gut ist mein Ruf?' ('How good is my Reputation?') (2012 / Gabal Verlag).

He looks forward to receiving your questions and feedback at michael.neubert@company2newmarket.com

Michael Neubert

Global Market Strategies

How to Turn Your Company into a
Successful International Enterprise

Translated from German by Myrna Lesniak

Campus Verlag
Frankfurt/New York

ISBN 978-3-593-39945-4

Contents

Introduction

Internationalizing companies and managing intercultural teams are more than ever part of the everyday life of employees and executives. Nevertheless, there are very few people with the right answers to the new challenges facing them today. As a result, the management of intercultural teams or international projects frequently ends in chaos when traditional methods are adopted. This not only endangers a manager's own career but also the successful internationalization or even the existence of the company. Consequently many of your colleagues ask the following questions:

- How can I develop a successful international strategy?
- How can I organize my international activities efficiently?
- How can I select overseas markets that are growing and will be profitable?
- How can I obtain correct and reliable information on overseas markets?
- How can I be successful with my products in the overseas markets selected?
- How can I develop these sales markets efficiently and how can I find new customers there?
- How can I manage intercultural (project) teams?
- How can I communicate efficiently with external stakeholders from other cultures?
- How can I benefit from free-trade agreements and how do I deal with political risks?
- How can I prevent errors and risks abroad from endangering the parent company?
- How can I reduce investments and the risks of financial loss abroad?

The following pages will provide you with answers to these and many other questions. The answers are backed up by sound theory and have been thoroughly tried and tested in practice. The *GMM Global Management Model,* which I have developed and implemented successfully over the years, focuses on the current practical demands placed on you and your colleagues. Whereas 5-10 years ago it was mainly specialized global managers of large companies that had anything to do with internationalizing, most employees nowadays, independent of their position in the hierarchy, have links with overseas. And that is only the beginning. Increasingly, skills such as dealing with other cultures and developing new markets are at least part of the standard repertoire of any ambitious manager. For that reason I have written this book for all those whose job actively involves international business or who expect to work in a state- or privately-owned organization whether as an employee, a student or an executive.

Many SMEs (small and medium sized companies) in Germany, Austria and Switzerland owe their export successes, among other things, to the *GMM Global Management Model* and have advanced to global market leaders in their market niches. Today, they are referred to as the so-called "hidden champions" in the field of globalization. As a result they set an example to many other SMEs and in conjunction with these are a reason for the export successes achieved by Germany, Austria and Switzerland. Numerous case studies can help you to recognize the factors needed for your success and to understand how using the *GMM Global Management Model* your company can become a champion of globalization whether you come from Brazil, Russia, India, China, North America, Africa or the Middle East.

The *GMM Global Management Model* provides you with a tool box that has been tried and tested for many years and enables you to manage and develop an international organization. You recognize opportunities and challenges more quickly and you acquire the skills to react to these in the appropriate manner. Your intercultural awareness is enhanced and by collaborating with new stakeholders you learn to operate at an international level. You continue to develop in a wholly targeted way, look for ever new and better solutions and adapt continuously to new challenges.

"Global Market Strategies" provides a comprehensive management model. From global vision to developing an internationalization strategy, from selecting and entering the foreign market to dealing with cultures and managing a global organization – the most important tasks and tools for you as a global manager are described in detail and with solutions and practical implementation in mind.

"Global Market Strategies" does not propagate simple solutions "for all". Unlike traditional guidebooks this reference book does not offer simple solutions of the kind "one size fits all" but deals methodically with complex, international questions that differ clearly from each other depending on the various companies and foreign markets.

"Global Market Strategies" does not pursue the latest fashions. That applies both to individual overseas markets and management methods. Deciding in favor of internationalization or a particular foreign market has a lasting impact on a company. Decisions that are wrong can threaten its very existence. Global managers make better decisions if they use both down-to-earth and well-tried methods and a professional approach.

"Global Market Strategies" offers high user value. The model is a combination of well-tried theories and comprehensive practical experience. It does not omit unpleasant topics such as market exit or corruption. That is why it is a realistic compass to help you negotiate the dynamic jungle of global opportunities and the risks entailed.

The structure of the book follows the steps to be found in the *GMM Global Management Model*. The first chapter addresses current trends, innovations and experiences in designing international corporate strategies. There is also a section on global competitive strategies.

The second chapter gives a detailed description of the management process "*company2newmarket*" for the successful opening of new foreign markets and thus deals entirely with the successful implementation of internationalization strategy. A key success factor is the *IMM International Market Monitor*. This early warning instrument and management information system supplies you with high-quality facts that form an objective basis for decision-making.

International management is always intercultural management, too. Efficient intercultural communication is a key factor for the success of international companies and one of the focal points of the *GMM*. The third chapter addresses collaboration with employees from other cultures by employing a *cultural profile*. It is this collaboration that will help your company to improve its intercultural intelligence.

The *GMM Global Management Model* presented here can help you arrive at better decisions and help you manage your international organization more efficiently and more successfully:

- You acquire new customers in new foreign markets in less time, with lower risk and with a minimal use of (financial and human) resources.
- You open up new foreign markets and launch new products more quickly and successfully than your competitors.
- You manage multi-cultural teams more efficiently and thereby profit from the advantages afforded by diversity.
- You benefit from the advantages of location in the individual foreign markets by producing high quality at competitive prices.

Finally, you develop internationalization to one of your core competences or even to a sustainable competitive advantage for your company. That way you achieve a leading global and, above all, a profitable market position in your market niche.

Do not hesitate but take the first step by reading this book. Become a champion in the field of internationalization. I would love to hear from you – what progress you have made and what your experiences have been abroad. Questions are always welcome. I can be contacted at michael.neubert@company2newmarket.com.

1. Internationalization Strategies – Innovative Strategies for Successful and Flexible Exploitation of Global Change

The only constant is change. Driven by the development of modern communication and information technology global networking between states, companies and people is continually on the increase. In a multi-polar world, the resulting complexity can scarcely be overlooked, let alone understood or managed and this also has an impact on developing global market strategies and opening up new markets.

Companies and their global managers are subject to pressure for greater internationalization and global hype. Almost every week, there are reports in the trade press on new and even more attractive foreign markets. Whereas BRIC and TRIADE countries have been a must for the location repertoire of every sensible global manager for some time, it is considered to be cool and hip today to make use of the growth potential of the Next11 and to explore the opportunities presented by the continent of Africa. This market-hopping may well promote the circulation of a magazine, but it very rarely impacts a company's balance sheet.

Every international company requires a very long-term perspective that also admits of setbacks. It is particularly dangerous if there are panic-stricken market exits and investment stops when the results that were expected fail to materialize immediately. Thus, many companies have come to a standstill somewhere in their internationalization process. They are faced with the ruins of their internationalization. Their subsidiaries are more like zombies that are more dead than alive but are languishing in foreign markets without any perspective. The only organizational unit that still continues to thrive magnificently is the group holding.

If subsidiaries withdraw from the market or companies turn their backs on internationalization, the group holdings often lose their raison d'être.

Nevertheless, in most cases there is no one there who has the courage or skill to assume responsibility for the further expansion of overseas activities. As a result, there will still be only a very limited number of companies implementing global internationalization strategies consistently and successfully.

A prerequisite for successful internationalization is having a clear international vision and strategy. This long-term decision is reached by the owners and it shapes and alters a company for a long time. Both the owners and the management need to be aware of the consequences of this decision; they need to want this decision; they need to be prepared to learn and also to stand by their decision even in difficult times. The method of "Let's give it a try" doesn't work.

Moving abroad also means that a company is venturing into new foreign markets where it is not familiar with the legal systems, networks, customers and suppliers. In cases of doubt, personal experience and knowledge count for little in these markets. Consequently, a company needs professional tools to enable it to meet these challenges. This first chapter addresses the current major tools, the trends, and the approaches for developing an internationalization strategy.

1.1. Preparing for Internationalization

Moving abroad requires thorough preparation. At the start of this process a company needs to ask itself what its international vision is in the long term, what short and medium term objectives this step means and what skills, competences and resources are available or will be required. Preparation for internationalization can be compared to preparation for a sports competition. At the end, the company is ready and in a position to prevail in global competition

The first condition for moving abroad is developing an international vision. This is the basis for an internationalization strategy and a key management instrument for global managers. It helps them to establish a good international reputation in terms of culturally adequate, authentic, honest and reliable conduct.

The second step entails defining internationalization objectives whereby it is important in this case to distinguish basically between objectives that are geared towards strategy, sales, efficiency and resources. Usually internationalization objectives vary depending on the industry and the business model. One conventional internationalization objective is the positioning of the company as a market leader in a clearly defined market niche and defending or expanding this by developing competitive advantages with this objective in mind.

This is then followed by taking stock of the appropriate competences and skills. This network of competences provides the basis for an international business model and as a competitive advantage it ought to be unique, sustainable and relevant and above all transferable abroad. Apart from the awareness of one's own strengths and weaknesses in addition to the opportunities and risks, the analysis of one's own business model always comprises a comparison with competitors.

Finally every company faces the decision whether it really should venture into new foreign markets or not. For this purpose, it is important to recognize the degree of internationalization desired and the ability of one's own industry to internationalize, and to deduce realistic alternative courses of action from this.

Developing a Global Corporate Vision

Developing a global corporate vision or mission is a crucial basis and condition for internationalizing any company. It describes how a company sees itself, where it stands and where it aims to go. "We are the world's leading providers of …….. technology for ……. solutions in the field of …." is a traditional corporate vision, which provides all stakeholders with all the relevant information on the company in one sentence.

This corporate vision serves as a guideline for employees no matter where they work and no matter what their culture or nationality is. It forms the basis for communication with all stakeholders outside the company, as well as with personal family and friends, with customers or suppliers. Information is motivation. A clear corporate vision gives them a sense of security and stability because then they know what objectives they are working for and they know that the company has come to their country to stay. This last point is particularly crucial for the motivation of local employees and executives, who are always afraid that a company will withdraw from the foreign market very quickly if it fails or that it is only making use of short-term advantages in a "hit and run" strategy.

For the management and its executives, a global corporate vision is the basis and the guideline on which an internationalization strategy is developed and also implemented of course (see Fig. 1). Deciding on a corporate vision takes precedence over the internationalization strategy; it functions as a steering mechanism for all activities of a global management model and is thus a prerequisite for all aspects of opening up new international markets. A corporate vision which is clear and well expressed has a positive impact on the motivation and commitment of all the executives and employees, and all stakeholders outside the company.

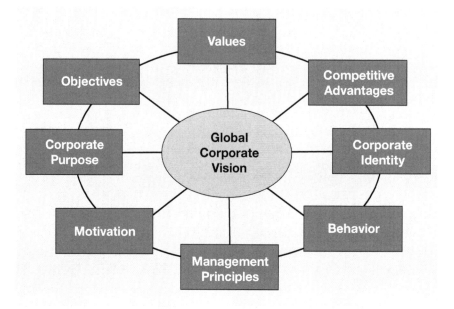

Fig 1: Elements of a global corporate vision

A corporate vision comprises international values, leadership values, the way to deal with external and internal stakeholders, and the purpose and identity of a company. Thus it defines the conduct that is desired in its employees and executives and gives numerous instructions and specifications for management situations, whether they are serious (for example: dealing with corruption) or intercultural (for example: the structure of remuneration schemes). Finally, a corporate vision also manifests itself in corporate communication, in corporate behavior and its corporate design.

A corporate vision applies to the whole of the international company; that means to all the international branch offices and subsidiaries. A corporate vision (apart from occasional common events) is often the only opportunity, especially for employees working far from headquarters, to establish a degree of identification with the entire company and to promote a sense of belonging.

It is precisely in an intercultural environment that a corporate vision is a crucial guide for global managers. Frequently, as far as local employees are concerned, the only representatives that companies have abroad are global managers. At the same time they are very far from head office where the company culture and values are practiced and demonstrated by the management daily. Consequently they need efficient instruments. A management handbook is a good example for it contains management culture and values based on the corporate vision and culture. The aim of this management handbook is the integration of all the employees independent of their origins and their culture into a uniform corporate and management culture.

At the same time a distinction is made between more "technical" and more "person-centered" corporate functions. Technical corporate functions are for example the fields of finance, project management, IT or compliance (including IP protection) that on a global level can be more readily standardized. Person-centered corporate functions include communication, marketing, sales, and customer services, which require considerable adaptation to the culture of the country in question.

Therefore a corporate vision is not an end in itself for the global manager but a key management instrument. That applies in particular to market entry forms based on collaboration with local partners in foreign markets (e.g. joint ventures), to integrating acquisitions in foreign countries or in markets with great cultural, geographical and structural (i.e. economical and administrative) distance.

Definition of International Corporate Objectives

Before developing an international corporate vision the owners ought to consider in detail the reasons for going abroad. This may sound banal but it isn't. Many companies tend to allow themselves to be driven willy-nilly into moving abroad, drawn by their customers (or other opportunities) and pushed into it by colleagues at the business roundtable talking of their great success in the new growth markets.

It seldom happens that international corporate objectives are clearly formulated. It is even rarer for companies to have any idea of what lies in store for them if they move abroad. Implementing an internationalization strategy will have a radical impact on the company. This can lead to more success but in cases of doubt it can also put the entire company at risk.

The question about international corporate objectives is more than legitimate; answering it is very important. Why does a company move abroad, where it doesn't know the market, the culture, the language or the political and legal framework conditions and where it has no customers? Potential, local customers don't know its brand or its products, its competitive advantages and services. Does a company intend to generate above-average returns for its owners under such conditions? After

---

Resources- and procurement oriented internationalization objectives

- Access to raw materials (valuable and in short supply)
- Access to knowledge, specific competences and experts
- Access to (cheap) capital

Sales oriented internationalization objectives

- Acquiring new profitable customers in new attractive foreign markets
- Retaining (and expanding) current customer relations that already exist abroad
- Extending the life cycle of established standard technologies and existing products
- Circumventing tariff and non-tariff trade barriers (for example: local-content or joint venture regulations) in order to gain access to the market in the first place
- Looking after existing export customers locally

Efficiency oriented internationalization objectives

- Using cost advantages (e.g. lower labor and energy costs or state subsidies)
- Expanding cost leadership by implementing the effects of cost and experience curves through higher sales volume
- Diversifying risks (e.g. exchange rates, fluctuations in demand, burdens due to taxes/ fees, and regulation)

Strategy oriented internationalization objectives

- Implementing an international corporate vision (e.g. establishing a leading global corporate position)
- Reacting to the activities of competitors (e. g. market entry by a foreign low-cost manufacturer)
- Establishing and developing core competences and competitive advantages that can be exploited globally

Table 1: Internationalization objectives

all, that sounds rather ambitious and not very realistic. Nevertheless, the urge to expand to foreign countries is enormous. As a result, companies pursue the objectives listed in Table 1.

In the past, *resource and procurement oriented reasons* were the major force behind the internationalization of companies. Today, this still applies to certain industries such as oil, natural gas and other energy companies or to certain company functions. For that reason, software companies outsource some of their programming departments to countries which have a knowledge or know-how that is not available in their own country. Companies from capital-intensive industries and from countries with inefficient capital markets (for example: primary commodity producers in mining or oil production for example) go to the biggest capital markets (for example: New York, London) to obtain the necessary financial resources at attractive conditions.

Nowadays, companies look for a way to enter new foreign markets especially when they would like to acquire new customers or sales markets or to strengthen or expand existing customer relations. The traditional global business model for *sales oriented* internationalization objectives is the "global exporter". The head office in the home country is responsible for the products which are sold via distribution subsidiaries or branch offices. As success in the market increases, assembly and services are relocated to the various foreign markets.

Implementing *efficiency oriented* internationalization objectives is mainly about benefiting from cost advantages and diversifying risks. Traditional cost advantages are wage and energy costs and subsidies for investment costs (for example: direct payments, depreciations, and tax advantages). These are also referred to as arbitrage objectives. By producing goods at more cost-effective locations and selling them at the market price in high-cost countries a company can improve its relative cost position and become more profitable.

Strategic internationalization objectives are gaining increasingly in significance. For this purpose the company adopts a holistic and global perspective in order to pursue more than just regional or non-market-specific objectives. In point of fact relations between the commitments in the different foreign markets ought to be increasingly born in mind. Examples of strategic internationalization objectives are establishing a global market position or worldwide competitive advantages, developing an international competitive strategy or implementing learning effects or economies of scales and scope.

Analysis of One's Own Business Model and Competitive Position

Before moving abroad every company should know its strengths and weaknesses. That is the only way it can decide with which products and competitive advantages it intends to enter the new foreign market or which knowledge and which skills are still required if internationalization is to be successful.

Taking Stock of and Outlining One's Own Competences and Competitive Advantages

After the corporate vision and the internationalization objectives have been established, an internal analysis is made about which resources are already available for implementation and which are still required.

Every company has resources. These are finance, people, organizations or technologies which become competences when implemented in certain combinations. This can be the ability to produce the product at a low price and of good quality, or it can be the knowledge and experience needed for solving customers' problems or handling customer situations. A core competence is an activity in the core processes which a company executes better than its competitors. A core competence becomes a competitive advantage if it creates greater customer benefits and /or offers these at lower costs (see Fig. 2). Competitive advantages that are used as a basis for internationalization need to be sustainable in the specific target markets, difficult to copy (in the case of knowledge it needs to be also protectable), profitable and above all they need to be of relevance to the local customers. Moreover, customers need to be prepared, in the long term, to pay a price which, from the company's point of view, is profitable.

According to Michael Porter's concept of the "competitive advantages of nations" companies develop skills in various countries or regions on account of the infrastructure there (for example: universities), the geo-

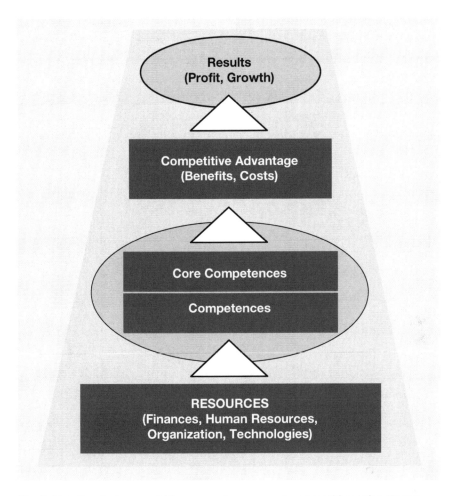

Fig 2: Relation between skills, competences and competitive advantages

graphy (for example: natural resources, tourism) or the history; they develop skills which do not exist in this form in other countries. Thus a manual or technical skill never amounts to a competitive advantage in the home country but it can definitely meet with brisk and profitable demand abroad (for example: Italian fashion). The reason for this is often to be found in the high level of competition which historically has forced all the local competitors to acquire and build up unique skills. It is quite possible that global competitive advantages can evolve from the competitive skill which has thus developed.

To begin with, a global manager ought, therefore, to make a list of all the skills and then assess to what extent these can be transferred to other countries. This list – or even better would be the word network – of the core competences and competitive advantages that can be transferred (see Fig. 3) is a significant indicator of the capacity for internationalization of the business model and of the willingness of foreign customers to pay an appropriate price for the products and services of the company.

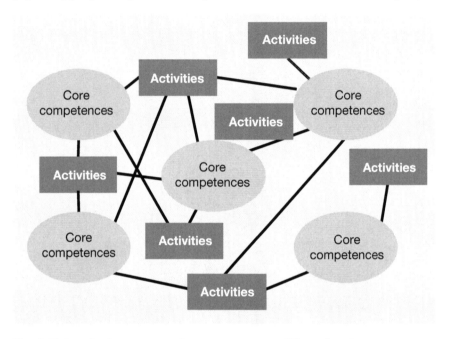

Fig. 3: Network of core competences as a competitive advantage

Transferring One's Own Competitive Advantages to New Foreign Markets

The simplest and best known instrument for answering the question as to whether a company can make use of its own competitive advantages and competences to take advantage of the opportunities presented in foreign markets is the SWOT analysis (Strengths, Weaknesses, Opportunities, Threats; see Fig 4). This is compiled from the point of view of each individual country and comprises not only the home markets but also all foreign and target markets. Thus a multi-dimensional picture emerges that furthermore contains external and internal perspectives with their strengths, weaknesses, opportunities and threats.

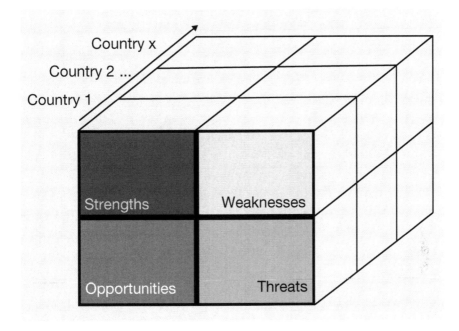

Fig. 4: Individual SWOT analysis for each foreign market

The evaluation examines whether there are strengths (or competences) within the entire company to be able to take advantage of the opportunities in decidedly diverse countries and target markets. Of course, the SWOT analysis cannot simply be made in an internal workshop but is supplemented with external data. In this way a global manager receives a rough idea initially as to whether the company's own competitive advantages can be transferred to foreign markets. In practice, answers are given for instance to the following questions on this subject: Do your own products have a competitive advantage in the target market? Is the company also competitive price-wise despite logistics and co-ordinations costs?

Analysis of the International Competitiveness of a Company

Apart from the tools already mentioned, Michael Porter's process, in three stages, for analyzing the international competitiveness of a company is widely used (see Fig. 5). The analysis begins at the economic level where the competitiveness of a company is analyzed within the framework conditions of its home country. The second stage concentrates on the competitive structure of the industry involved. In this connection an analysis is made as to which of the Five Forces will be in a long-term position to generate the highest return on equity with their activities in the value chain. This information enables each company to find a competitive market position, which it can defend against the other Five Forces with its competences and competitive advantages.

It is not until the final stage that the company's value chain is analyzed (for example: the competitive triangle) and compared individually with other competitors (for example: benchmarking, best practice-analyses). In particular, two parameters – the cost of and the customer benefits from the product – are used in this comparison. This concerns increasing customer benefits and improving the cost position by increasing productivity and lowering costs and aims to identify the core competences and the weak points in the various activities. The latter are outsourced to specialists whose core competences are precisely these activities.

The success of many international companies lies mostly in the competitive advantages they have achieved in their home markets through framework conditions and the high level of competition. In a precise analysis, networks of manufacturers, suppliers and customers are often to be found which, depending on the foreign market, are referred to as industrial clusters: e.g. Chaebol (in Korea) or Keiretsu (in Japan). Industrial clusters are characterized by good contacts and close connections to the companies in an industry. In addition they have all the necessary resources such as capital, natural resources or qualified employees to establish a high level of competitiveness. There is any number of famous examples: the technology firms in Silicon Valley and Route 128 in the USA, the IT/software industry in the Bangalore region in India, the clothing industry in North Italy or trading with raw materials in Geneva and Zug in Switzerland.

Global managers can derive their internationalization strategy solely from the origin of a company. Frequently, therefore, industrial clusters

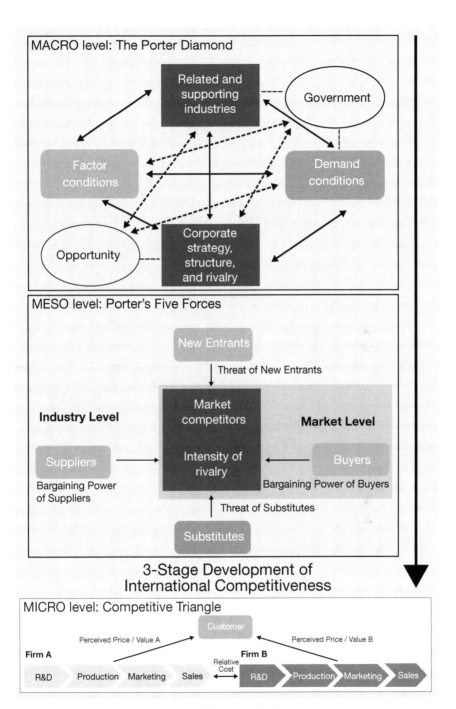

MACRO level: The Porter Diamond

Related and supporting industries

Government

Factor conditions

Demand conditions

Opportunity

Corporate strategy, structure, and rivalry

MESO level: Porter's Five Forces

New Entrants

Threat of New Entrants

Industry Level

Market competitors

Market Level

Suppliers

Intensity of rivalry

Buyers

Bargaining Power of Suppliers

Bargaining Power of Buyers

Threat of Substitutes

Substitutes

3-Stage Development of International Competitiveness

MICRO level: Competitive Triangle

Customer

Perceived Price / Value A

Perceived Price / Value B

Firm A

Firm B

Relative Cost

R&D Production Marketing Sales

R&D Production Marketing Sales

Fig. 5: Establishing global competitiveness in three stages

jointly expand their entire value chain abroad. Thus competitive advantages arise from the networks with suppliers, major customers and distribution channels.

Finally, the three stages of this analyzing process are an aid to discovering hitherto unknown markets and to understanding which activities enable the individual competitors to actually earn money. Frequently, these are innovative customer benefits. The search for new business fields is referred to as "blue ocean strategy". The engineering industry is a good example of this. At first the companies in this industry concentrated solely on developing, producing and distributing their products. Today, services such as financing or maintenance contracts are a key source of sales and proceeds. This also applies to airlines, who due to the high level of competitiveness could hardly earn money from their core business of providing transport services. Thus Miles & More, the customer retention program, is no longer a cost factor for Lufthansa meanwhile, but a very profitable line of business.

Deciding to Internationalize

A company is now in a position to develop realistic alternative courses of action for its own internationalization independent of its own industry and skills.

Developing Alternative Courses of Action

At this point at the latest, global managers ought to have a precise idea of the internationalization objectives and be familiar with their competences and competitive advantages. Thus, they are in a position to develop alternative courses of action on the basis of two decision-making criteria using tools such as the two-dimensional nine-cell matrix (see Table 2). However, the matrix can also be reduced to four cells (for example: the Ansoff-Matrix) or even expanded to 16 cells. Global managers are free to choose the criteria. The two decision-making criteria chosen are the degree of internationalization of one's own industry as well as the ability and willingness to internationalize one's own company. On the one hand, the latter contains a global corporate strategy with international development objectives (willingness) and on the other hand, the necessary resources (finance, human resources, knowledge, organization, technologies) and competitive advantages that are the conditions for internationalization. This breakdown enables a realistic view of potential alternative courses of action and shows which tasks a company needs to tackle before actually undertaking internationalization.

		Degree of internationalization of one's own industry		
		Homeland	Regional	Global
Ability and willingness to internationalize one's own company	Willingness and ability	Diversification to a new business field	Preparing for globalization	Establishing & strengthening global market position
	Willingness	Preparing for regionalization	Global export as niche supplier	Searching for strategic alliances
	Non-existent	Penetrating home market	Regional export as niche supplier	Market exit (or sale)

Table 2: Nine-cell matrix for developing alternative courses of action

It is precisely those companies in industries with considerable international focus that face very realistic and, in many cases, very difficult decisions. If there is no willingness or ability to internationalize, then usually the only course is to exit the market. Even if a company succeeds in positioning itself in the short term, sales, profitability and the value of the company will decrease in the long term. On the other hand, entrepreneurs need to provide the necessary resources for globalizing their own company. It is this which in the beginning offers many opportunities but entails considerable risks, too.

Degree of Internationalization and Ability of a Company and of an Industry to Internationalize

The degree of internationalization of an industry or the ability of the individual company to internationalize depends to a large extent on the business model. An increase in internationalization has led to the concept of "born global" developing. It defines companies that are already international when they are founded or which internationalize shortly afterwards. These are principally innovative high technology firms in highly competitive industries that occupy their market niche on the global market as soon as possible in order to refinance their investments. Thus Apple, for example, (almost) simultaneously launches new product innovations on the worldwide market at increasingly shorter intervals. In addition the concept of "born-again globals" has developed also. These are well established companies that internationalize quickly and with specific objectives after successfully developing their home market.

The development of "born globals" is influenced favorably by various factors: the increasing significance of niche markets, the progress in process and production technology, the ability of small and medium-sized business to act swiftly, the progress in communications and information technology (for example: E and M commerce) and growing global networks. Although, under these conditions, internationalization can be accelerated, "born globals" do their homework, too, and use very structured market development processes (for example: "company2newmarket").

"Born globals" also develop in industries that have no or few barriers to entry into new foreign markets or where the cost of adapting products, services and processes is very low. Examples of these are producers of raw materials who sell worldwide, software manufacturers and service providers, and social media companies.

Companies with a mere, local competitive advantage cannot transfer this to another market. Thus, a London tour-guide's knowledge of monuments, restaurants and shortcuts is of no help to him should he move to Tokyo. On the contrary: he even has a market disadvantage because he has to acquire the necessary competences first. This also applies to strongly nationally regulated industries such as the financial services industry. Strong regulation restricts the exploiting of scale effects and curbs innovation, growth and profitability.

Despite these restrictions most companies have the potential to become a "born global" or a "hidden champion" (i.e. world leader in their own market niche). In this case, the global manager's qualifications and developing and implementing a professional internationalization strategy are paramount.

This chapter outlined the major preparations for moving abroad. For this purpose a company should have a clear, long-term idea of its own international activities, define its objectives in concrete terms and it should become familiar with itself again. It is particularly important to scrutinize one's own competences, competitive advantages and resources. On the basis of this information it is possible to develop alternative courses of action.

The ability and willingness to internationalize one's own company is based on the one hand on a global corporate vision with international development objectives and on the other hand on the availability of the necessary resources (finance, human resources, knowledge, organization, technologies) and competitive advantages. The experience and the ability of the corporate management are key factors in this case.

1.2. Core Elements of an Internationalization Strategy

A good internationalization strategy is vital for success abroad. Its core elements reflect current trends and developments and are a good indicator of successful implementation. They form the basis for moving abroad, the huge allocation of resources and sustainable organizational change. Unfortunately these are often thrown overboard in day-to-day operations, are qualified by "unique" opportunities or dominated by situational and emotional criteria. And so a major customer presses for market entry or the colleagues at the business round table call for more courage and farsightedness.

Apart from these reactive or passive market entry strategies this section will address active market entry strategies in particular. These are based on facts and form a foundation for decision-making. This also applies to the subsequent target market strategies, horizontal and vertical market entry strategies and the so-called market maturity strategies. The latter, for example, with the option theory, extension of the product life-cycle or the securing of resources such as raw materials and intellectual property show numerous up-to-date approaches which are also relevant in practice.

Active and Reactive Market Entry Strategies

Market entry strategies are either active or reactive. The former are sub-divided into market entry strategies that are market-research based, experience-based and option-based. A global manager needs to know them all in order to be successful in implementing an internationalization strategy on the one hand and taking advantage of the opportunities presented in the foreign markets on the other hand.

Reactive or Passive Market Entry Strategies

In a reactive market entry strategy, the decisive impulse for entering a foreign market does not come from the company itself but from an external stakeholder. Usually these are existing customers who in moving abroad force their suppliers to go along with them. The motivation is not to be found in the desire to internationalize but in the wish to maintain and secure an existing customer relationship. Reactive behavior can be observed primarily among suppliers (for example: suppliers to the

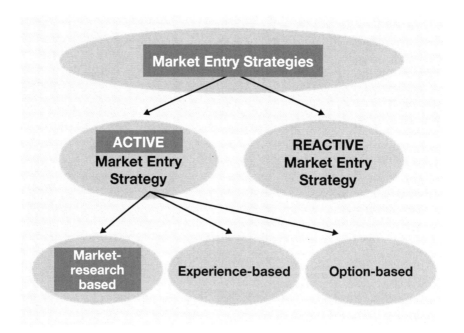

Fig. 6: Active and reactive market entry strategies

automobile industry) and companies providing services (for example: banks, insurances, consultants, accountants and advertising agencies).

This approach helps to maintain existing networks and value chains and the ensuing competitive advantages. Moreover, there is no need to compensate for an infrastructure that is missing in the foreign market. High-performance industrial clusters like the Chaebols in Korea, the Keiretsus in Japan or family-owned companies in China make intensive use of these advantages.

Using a reactive market entry strategy can definitely make sense because the attractiveness of a foreign market for a supplier depends to a large extent on the existence of customers. Thus, internationalization is virtually outsourced to the customers. This saves most of the costs of developing the market and avoids the risks involved. However, there is also an increase in the danger – for example after ending a customer relationship – of being stuck with a portfolio of unattractive foreign markets.

Active Market Entry Strategies

Option-based active market entry strategy: By using an option-based market entry strategy a company reacts to unique opportunities presented by international markets. A typical market opportunity is a country – driven by political change – that opens up to foreign investments. A well-known example of this is the dissolution of the former Warsaw Pact and the former Soviet Union in the late 80s and early 90s. Today opportunities may perhaps arise in foreign markets such as Cuba or Venezuela.

A further option is afforded by the liberalization of entire industries (for example: telecommunications, energy) or the sale of individual state-owned companies. Frequently the latter are local market leaders. This is an attractive and unique entry opportunity in what may prove to be a long-term attractive foreign market. Even the opportunity to buy up competitors, in as far as these were not "planned", is part of an option based market entry strategy.

Opportunities also present themselves in foreign markets as a result of external events such as new framework conditions in a foreign market (for example: lower political risks, liberal legislation, subsidies) or as a result of internal events (for example: employees who come from the target market, innovations). Opportunities and options are always unique occasions that only arise for a short period. A company can take advantage of these opportunities if it is in a position to make quick decisions and provide the necessary resources at short notice.

An option-based market entry strategy is appropriate for supplementing the market-research based market entry strategy. This integration is aimed at screening the attractiveness of the foreign market and compatibility with the existing market entry strategy before taking advantage of a unique opportunity. Thus the option-based market entry strategy is unsuitable as a sole course of action within the framework of an internationalization strategy.

Experience-based active market entry strategy: The experience-based active market entry strategy is based – as the name suggests – on the experiences of a company in the past, especially in its home market. Expansion is carried out gradually in foreign markets which have a cultural, structural and geographical proximity or relationship. As a rule, a market concentration strategy is pursued for this purpose whereby resources are concentrated on one market entry only. Further internationalization of these successfully developed foreign markets follows the same methodology. Thus a company internationalizes according to cultural, language, structural and even geographical criteria.

Of course, the experience-based market entry strategy only makes sense if there is a high degree of structural, cultural and geographic proximity because otherwise it is hardly possible to transfer experiences and competitive advantages. These framework conditions can be found for example in free-trade areas like the EU, NAFTA, DR-CAFTA or the GCC countries; in clusters like the Scandinavian countries and Oceania and also in regions with the same language skills as for example in the Commonwealth of Nations, between France and North Africa or between the Iberian Peninsula and Latin America.

The experience-based active market entry strategy is particularly appropriate for business models which need a high level of adjustment to customer requirements and buying patterns in the foreign market in question. Due to the cultural, structural and geographic proximity, it is easier to transfer experiences and competitive advantages. This applies especially to highly developed free-trade areas with harmonized legislation and free movement of capital and persons. "Born-global" business models such as social networks, producers of raw materials or techno-logical firms rarely tend to make use of this market entry strategy.

An experience-based active market entry strategy means that costs, risks and the time needed for projects to open up new markets can be reduced significantly. However, this means that even more attractive foreign markets in other regions of the world are never even identified and analyzed. Today, a company cannot afford to miss market opportunities. Therefore, the experience-based active market entry strategy is today becoming more and more part of the market-research based active market entry strategy.

Market-research based active market entry strategy: The market-research based active market entry strategy (see Fig. 7) is based on a structural and systematic approach whereby the most attractive foreign markets are selected according to clearly defined criteria. The market-research based active market entry strategy is implemented in a multi-stage market evaluation and selection process. This process aims at an efficient evaluation and selection of attractive and appropriate foreign markets. In practice, a three-stage process has proved to be sufficient although more or fewer stages can be used depending on the industry and the global manager's experience. The individual stages function like a filter which becomes progressively finer with each stage. The more attractive the foreign market is the more intensively it is analyzed. The basis is an efficient market information system such as the *IMM International Market Monitor*, with which major foreign markets are continually observed and which also functions as an early warning system for potential opportunities and risks.

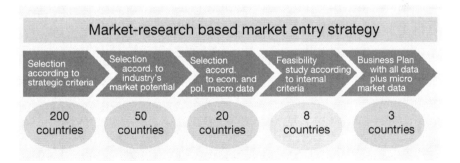

Fig. 7: Gradual market selection of a market-research based market entry strategy

The market-research based market entry strategy is appropriate for every company. It is the only market entry strategy that is based on objective criteria, that helps to develop alternative courses of action and serves as the basis for the management's decision-making. Often it is the smaller companies which regard this work-intensive approach with certain skepticism until they meet with the first negative experiences. Thus, a very practicable approach has been chosen in the chapters which follow so that attractive foreign markets can be selected most efficiently and at manageable cost.

It is important to clearly delimit "wellness and hanger-on strategies". In recent years, China was thus "in". It was a must to be up there with the rest and you could have a say both on the home market and on the target market, too. In China it is possible to meet up with a large home market community that might perhaps save a company the one or other experience. However, this approach has nothing to do with strategy and is rarely sustainable and usually not successful either.

Target Market Strategies

A target market strategy enables a company to select the foreign markets to be entered. A well-known tool for depicting the various target market strategies is the four-cell matrix according to Ansoff, which combines the two elements "target market" and "product". This matrix can be expanded to nine (see Fig. 8) or even 16 cells and can also be supplemented by a third dimension to enable flexible adaptation to the demands of a transnational internationalization strategy whereby the strategic alternative courses of action rise perceptibly from 4 to 27.

This expansion makes sense. Thus, it is possible to differentiate clearly between the new foreign markets with regard to their attractiveness, their membership in free-trade areas, and their cultural, structural or geographical proximity to the home market of the internationalizing company or with respect to political and economic risks. In addition, a further development of the home market is also an alternative. These differences increase the number of categories (for example on the X axis) and thus the alternative courses of action, too.

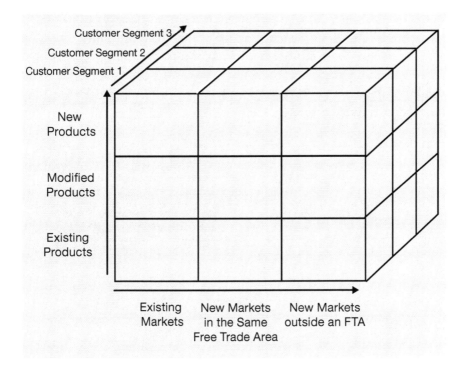

Fig. 8: Developing target market strategies on the basis of a three-dimensional matrix

In a so-called *market presence strategy* for example, companies concentrate entirely on a limited number of foreign markets, as for example on other member states in their free-trade area (for example: the EU, NAFTA, ASEAN or Mercosur), major emerging countries (for example: BRIC) or foreign markets with the strongest growth (for example: Growth8).

In a *market selection strategy* global managers select foreign markets according to their attractiveness, risks, investment costs or market entry barriers. At the same time they can combine a market presence strategy with a market selection strategy. After deciding in favor of a market presence in the EU they choose the most attractive foreign markets for development with, for example, a branch office as a market entry form and export their products to the less attractive foreign markets of the EU.

Within the framework of a *market segmentation strategy*, the most attractive target group is chosen from the list of the foreign markets selected. This can be done for one foreign market only (*intranational*) or in a cross-border strategy for several foreign markets (*transnational*) – but also for several regions. New, existing, or modified products and services are offered in the individual market segments. The choice is based on the culture of the foreign market and the buying patterns and preferences of the market segment targeted.

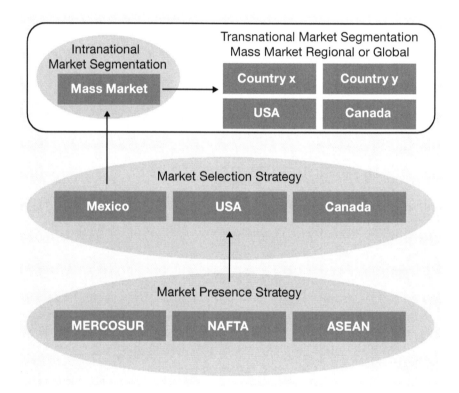

Fig. 9: Implementing a target market strategy

Horizontal versus Vertical Internationalization

A vertical expansion abroad is either geared towards a procurement market or a sales market. Its objective is to obtain competitive advantages by means of access to raw materials, lower production costs (lower factor costs or higher factor productivity) or to attractive sales markets. A company can also make use of these advantages by purchasing from a local manufacturer or selling his products via sales channels available in the market (exports). Setting up one's own production facilities and/or one's own distribution channels only makes sense if the external partners prove to be unreliable, the dependence on them becomes excessive or they fail to supply the necessary performance with regard to sales, service or quality. Examples are access to raw materials for technology companies or luxury fashion houses establishing their own shops.

This also applies to horizontal expansion abroad. This entails the parallel establishment of production facilities and of a distribution network in the target country or the establishment of a "copy" of the existing company in the target market. The forces behind such a decision are formidable barriers to market entry, avoidance of currency fluctuations, high transport costs or a high degree of adaptation to the specific target market. A good example was the setting up of car factories (BMW/Mercedes) in the USA so that production in the US-dollar area would reduce the disadvantage of being subject to currency fluctuations. The natural course of licensing or contract manufacturing was not an alternative because as far as BMW and Mercedes were concerned protecting the brand, their production technology, their know-how and their core competences had priority. Apart from that, the market entry form of licensing or contract manufacturing is a possible solution in less attractive markets with formidable barriers to market entry.

Market Maturity Strategies

There is a considerable difference in the levels of development in the individual foreign markets of an industry. This evaluation is always from the perspective of the company making the analysis (and from the perspective of the home market, too). The most crucial criterion is the transferability of one's own competences and competitive advantages to the foreign market in question.

A foreign market is regarded as more developed if the company's own competences are not sufficient to be able to succeed there. A foreign market is assessed as less or also equally developed if a company is able to establish local competitive advantages with its own competences and skills and achieve its internationalization objectives.

However, development in the individual foreign markets is seldom better or worse but usually different. One foreign market has a better logistics infrastructure, whereas the other has more efficient distribution channels or has an effective legal system. For that reason, an evaluation only provides useful results from the point of view of each individual company.

Fig. 10: Market maturity strategies

Market Entry Strategies in More Developed Markets

A company does not possess the necessary competences and skills for market entry into more developed foreign markets in order to be able to succeed there. Consequently, market entry is not, at first sight, interesting because the company's own competitive strengths are insufficient. If the attractiveness of this foreign market is strong, a company can compensate the lack of skills by choosing an appropriate market entry form (for example: a joint venture) and enter the market successfully after all.

Frequently, companies also have a strategic interest in more developed foreign markets. By acquiring a local market participant the company gains access to such resources as knowledge, skills, human resources, competences or raw materials, which can be used in the entire company or in all the foreign markets. These strategic acquisitions are part of a transnational internationalization strategy and help a company to increase its global competitiveness.

Market Entry Strategies into Less Developed Markets

Market entry into less developed markets is the norm. A company selects the foreign markets that are attractive and where it has considerable competitive strength. In this case, a whole range of actions, details of which are given in the chapters which follow, is available to the company. Apart from the traditional course of action there are two strategic approaches worth mentioning that are key elements of a transnational market entry strategy:

Extending the product life cycle: The strategy of "extending the product life cycle" means that the production of existing and established products that are approaching the end of their life cycle are transferred along with the manufacturing facilities to a less developed foreign market with a view to generating further profits from investments (already depreciated) and products.

Moreover, competitiveness improves perceptibly. Apart from a reduction in production costs products are adapted to the requirements, for example, of emerging countries. These entail less difficult operation methods (operating the machine is made easy to learn) and a greater robustness in the face of adverse circumstances (temperature fluctuations, damp, power fluctuations, the alternating quality of processed raw materials etc.). Thus high quality, locally adapted and cheaper products are developed that are competitive in emerging countries and probably in industrialized countries, too.

Companies with a transnational internationalization strategy go one step further: they also use this cost advantage in more developed foreign markets and offer these products worldwide too. Most companies do not recognize the potential afforded by this transnational internationalization strategy. Although they use the cost advantages of a product in emerging countries, they merely serve the local and, at best, the regional market with these products. Thus they never achieve the economies of scale of their local competitors and consequently they retain their cost disadvantage in this foreign market. An improvement in their cost position is only possible if they sell the products produced there worldwide and that means on their home market, too.

The "Real-Option" Theory: The "Real-Option" Theory is decisive in clarifying a real growth option in a target market. Options are particularly valuable in (still) unattractive target markets – i.e. in cases of uncertainty. This is illustrated very impressively by the example of VW in China. It was due to their early entry into what was then a still unattractive Chinese market that VW had a real option or the opportunity to gain market leadership. Today, VW profits from its strong market position and, compared with its competitors, can compensate the sales crisis in Europe in excellent fashion. This example shows that the value of the option rises congruent with the market risk. The logic of the "Real-Option" Theory contradicts the market-research based market entry strategy, which is founded on the current attractiveness of the market and one's own competitive strength, but gains in attractiveness and significance in today's volatile times. Nevertheless, it must be remembered that options are only opportunities that unfortunately are often wasted or that entail meeting unpleasant funding obligations.

The active market-research based market entry strategy within the framework of a transnational internationalization strategy is often selected as the further course of action. It is only here that the economies of scope and scale, and the synergies for example of a geocentric and intercultural HR policy can unfold. Diversity – and its exploitation – is thus the core of every transnational internationalization strategy and leaves its mark on all strategic and operative decision-making processes. Nevertheless, the option- and experience-based market entry strategy as an addition is justified. Opportunities ought to be seized at all times, but only in attractive markets.

This also applies to target market strategies that in market selection and (transnational) market segmentation are based entirely on the facts provided by a market-research based process for market evaluation and selection. Market maturity strategies also show the advantages of the transnational internationalization strategy. The global utilization of scarce resources and cost advantages increase competitiveness perceptibly. Thus companies succeed in finding ways into almost every attractive foreign market.

1.3. Developing a Flexible Global Organizational Structure

The company is now ready to develop its internal organizational structure. It has a clear long-term and international corporate vision and market entry strategy, knows its own competences, competitive advantages and resources and has examined the capacity of its business model for internationalization. Furthermore, the corporate management and the global manager, too, have the necessary skills, experience and also the willingness which is a key condition for developing new foreign markets successfully.

In designing processes and organization a company is constantly trying to strike a balance between "local responsiveness" and "global integration" and between centralization and decentralization. This requires the skill to increase the efficiency of an international organization with synergies and symbioses instead of achieving the opposite with simple compromises. Only international companies that manage to overcome these extremes and exploit them are successful in the long term. They take into account a few of the basic organizational design elements of transnational organizations that can be transferred to most industries and companies.

It is to this end that the SPOT (strategy, processes, organization and technology) method is employed. First of all, the strategy is developed, then the processes are defined and the organization built up in order to achieve the strategic objectives. The value chain provides an appropriate tool for this purpose. Due to its flexibility and its reputation, it permits the simple and transparent representation of the various types of processes for and the place for the production of goods and services.

Transnational Organizational Structures and Dealing with Extremes

The organizational structure of a company is always based on its strategy. This also applies to international organizations. Although SMEs' often still functional organizational structures are very successful, MNEs (multi-national enterprises) rely increasingly on transnational organization forms.

Local Adaptation versus Global Integration

Coping with apparently irreconcilable extremes is a core task of the global manager and affects, for example, the question of whether to standardize or not as opposed to differentiating between products, services, processes and all the other activities of an international company or dealing with other cultures.

There are no "either or" solutions. There are good arguments in favor of both extremes with the result that these can lead to lengthy discussions. However, the one strategy cannot work without the other. So far, global products that have been standardized for and launched on global markets have scarcely been successful; the same applies to completely differentiated conglomerates. Cheap compromises do not lead to the objective either. Consequently, it is the global manager's task to recognize the advantages of both organizational alternatives and to connect them synergistically to each other.

Meanwhile, successful multi-national companies have mastered the art of reconciling opposites. They make use of the advantages and opportunities of the diversity between markets and cultures and look for the best employees and locations worldwide to implement them. This geocentric approach is the basis for establishing a transnational organizational structure and especially for implementing a transnational internationalization strategy.

Centralizing versus Decentralizing

The contrast between centralizing and localizing tasks, competences and responsibilities among a central holding and its regional or national subsidiaries is often at the root of inefficient organizations and growing political discussions.

It is international companies in particular that are always alternating between centralizing and decentralizing. As soon as a company looks for more growth, the regional or national subsidiaries are usually given more scope for adapting products and processes locally. As soon as a subsidiary fails to make successful use of the freedom it has gained, the central controlling and centralizing reflexes take hold immediately ... and everything starts all over again.

Establishing and developing local subsidiaries can be compared to the relationship between a mother and child. Children always remain children as far as the mother is concerned, no matter their age. She finds it difficult to give them their independence so that they can gain their own experiences. But a subsidiary requires independence if it is to be successful. As it increases in size and becomes more successful, it becomes more and more integrated into its market and becomes an increasingly better "good corporate citizen". Whereas a mother is primarily interested in the well-being of her children and is proud when they develop well, managers at headquarters are seldom voluntarily prepared to decentralize and give up competences. This unwillingness usually results in an immediate stagnation of foreign sales and to further centralization on account of the lack of success. In the end this vicious circle causes the internationalization strategy to fail unless an experienced global manager steps in and puts an end to it. Unfortunately this kind of behavior (at headquarters etc.) can be observed much too frequently. *The failure of internationalization strategies is seldom due to the market but usually to people's vanity.*

A global manager will be successful if he can obtain entrepreneurial and experienced country managers for the regional and national subsidiaries, integrate these and their skills into the decision-making and planning processes (for example for in- and outsourcing or off-shoring), and provides them with the necessary "air cover" to develop the market successfully.

Global Configuration and Co-ordination of Physical and Virtual Activities

The global co-ordination of all physical and virtual activities is an enormous challenge to a global manager. It can be seen clearly in Fig. 11, which has been simplified radically to include only four different stages of the value chain, that, apart from the known physical value creation process, attention should be paid to virtual value creation processes for processing information, and developing services and individual customer projects. In addition, there are the various support processes by staff departments as well as management processes for operating the global organization.

Due to its adaptability and prominence the value chain is an ideal instrument for depicting the procedural implementation of a transnational

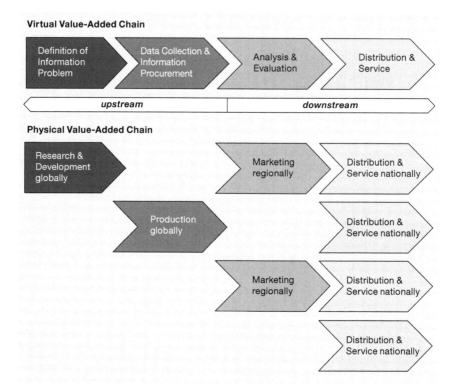

Fig. 11: Physical and virtual value chains

internationalization strategy because it includes the four organizational design elements. The individual activities of the value chain are implemented at the place where the highest competence and the highest cost efficiency exist. This is not always the head office.

In foreign markets, competitive advantages emerge from establishing local competences and local barriers to market entry. At headquarters, competitive advantages arise from the economies of scale and scope which originate, however, in the activities in the individual foreign markets. The global manager can influence the development of competitive advantages with clever configuration (organization of the value chain) and coordination (management of the value chain).

There is a perceptible difference in the infrastructure in the various foreign markets. Instead of using one's own valuable and meager resources to build up the infrastructure that is missing a company ought to import the primary products and services from other foreign markets or encourage suppliers to offer these locally, too.

It is precisely in foreign markets that the value chain is not a linear but an iterative, cyclical process to be able to take advantage of customers' problems and market opportunities, too. Thus competitive advantages arise from the skill and competence to solve customers' problems. Virtual value chains for processing information and solving customers' problems arise parallel to this whereby added value arises from the processing of information. Today this is used for example by external consultants such as strategy consultants, accountants and solicitors. Internally, information-based value creation processes are also used for reducing costs (for example: CIP), for customer care (for example: CRM) or for developing new products. For that reason services are becoming more and more important for industrial companies.

Organizational Design Elements of Transnational Organizational Structures

Today, multi-national companies have a geocentric perspective, with which they pursue strategic internationalization objectives. This transnational internationalization strategy is based on the worldwide utilization of the advantages of different locations (arbitrage), the use of global technology and product platforms (aggregation), the adaptation of the marketing mix to the national requirements of customers and culturally specific buying patterns (adaptation), the ability to understand changes in international markets (analysis) and the acquiring of geocentric personnel and resources. This also includes the global co-ordination of all value creation activities.

The transnational internationalization strategy ought to always concentrate on maximizing the benefits of the customer in question because cultures and markets still consist of people and not products. To be sure there are such things as global products but there are no global people and cultures (as yet).

Adaptation of Products and Services to Local Markets

The automotive industry is an absolute master at adapting products to local markets. Thus, on the same technology platform there are various brands and models which, depending on customers' wishes and the legislation of a country, vary in their features, their guarantee and services. The situation is similar in the consumer goods industry. Adaptation of products to the local market is restricted to the elements of the marketing mix. Therefore, packaging sizes, promotional materials or marketing channels are adapted to customers' requirements and buying patterns whereas the technology or formula are not touched. Chain restaurants, too, adapt their existing products or complement their product range depending on local taste and eating habits with the result that the menu is not identical in any country.

The aim of this (expensive) adaptation to the local markets is to establish a good market position, if possible as one of the market leaders, or put quite simply: to achieve more sales. Although, in the case of retail products and consumer goods local adaptation has gone a long way, this is frequently not enough in countries where the culture is very different. Thus many companies – if they cannot resign themselves to being niche players – have no alternative but to acquire a local competitor and use his expertise to become familiar with local consumers.

Local adaptation is mainly restricted to the instruments of the marketing mix because the technological platform or the formula of a product can only be interfered with in a very limited way on account of the global economies of scope and scale.

Distribution and marketing costs vary in the different industries and countries. Whereas they amount to approx. 2–5 % for example in financial services, they are 30 to 40 % in the automotive industry, 40 % in the publishing industry and frequently over 50 % in the clothing industry. Thus considerable importance is attached to the choice of an appropriate distribution and marketing strategy for each market. The number of and kind of distribution channels is usually limited within a country so that under certain circumstances the pressure to adapt is considerable.

Alternatively, a company can decide to set up its own distribution channel. Although this increases independence, this constitutes a long-term and resource-intensive project especially with respect to personal and shop-based sales. It is those companies with limited resources that avoid such a high investment risk and in addition listed companies avoid the long time that such a course requires. Frequently they switch to modern distribution channels like E-commerce and direct marketing.

Developing Product and Service Platforms

By developing product and service platforms international companies try to maximize sales globally or sell the largest possible quantities of a broadly identical product and thus expect economies of scale and scope for example in the field of production costs, R & D, global branding or product quality.

Car makers are the best example of utilizing platform strategy. They use the same technical platforms for a vast number of brands and models. In this way they succeed in apportioning the development costs to the high quantities of one product and lowering the average production costs. Today, the platform strategy is used in almost every suitable industry because the R & D costs and the fierceness of competition are so great and technology cycles are so short that profitable refinancing is generally only possible via immediate, global marketing.

Utilizing Global Advantages

The utilization of global advantages is based on the idea that various foreign markets have advantages which the home country, the current production location or the various sales markets do not have. These advantages can pertain to all the resources or aspects of a foreign market as for example:

- Lower costs of labor, land, capital or energy;
- Subsidies in the form of direct or indirect grants or tax savings;
- Access to knowledge and skills or well-trained employees;
- Access to other resources such as raw materials;
- Access to local sales markets by avoiding tariffs and high logistics costs;
- Access to international sales markets via membership in a free-trade area or a large number of free-trade agreements;
- Utilization of the infrastructure such as traffic and universities or tax advantages.

When a production location is being selected, the realization of economies of scale speaks for selecting a central location whereas the savings of logistics costs, a short delivery period and better adaptability to local requirements and preferences speak for decentralized production locations. Thus in the case of large and heavy products with low production costs the economies of scale are quickly compensated by the logistics costs. In contrast, the logistics costs of software can be ignored so that in this case the location advantages of a foreign market will be fully realized.

In a multi-stage production process, it is possible to unite the advantages of centralized and decentralized production. Thus basic components are produced on a centralized basis at an appropriate location or purchased from a supplier, whereas assembly and delivery are carried out on a decentralized basis for a region (for example: free-trade area) or on a national basis for a foreign market. This cross-border integrated production makes systematic use of the advantages of location and specialization in the individual markets. The company benefits from the economies of scale and the relative location advantages on the one hand and from the adaptation to local sales markets on the other hand. However, potential logistics problems, state regulations (e.g. local content) or different quality standards may have an adverse effect.

A distinction is also made in purchasing between centralized "single sourcing" and decentralized "local sourcing". Whereas economies of scale such as cost degression and quantity discounts speak for centralization, the advantages of decentralization are lower transport costs, shorter delivery periods or lower environmental pollution. Moreover, better integration into the local market speaks for decentralization. It is precisely the companies that come from industrial clusters and whose competitive advantages depend largely on their contacts and connection to suppliers and distribution channels that internationalize with their entire value chain. They bring along their own infrastructure with, among other things, their own distribution channels and suppliers.

Today, every company reeling under massive cost and pricing pressure looks for a little more revenue and growth. It is only with a transnational organizational structure that companies today can make full use of all the economies of scope and scale. A precondition for this is always a geocentric perspective and diversity in all corporate divisions. In this case, for example in HR policy, the most suitable employees are always recruited independent of their origin, nationality or culture.

A transnational organizational structure always consists of three elements: utilizing cost advantages, establishing global product, market and technology platforms and adapting to local market requirements. In addition, there is the global co-ordination and structuring of value chains. Thus, alleged extremes between cultures or between centralizing and decentralizing, and global integration and local adaptation are combined both symbiotically and synergistically. This is practiced successfully by a growing number of companies. This means that in the meantime the transnational organizational structure has become a condition for competitiveness in tomorrow's global markets.

1.4. Implementing Competitive Strategies

Timing strategies are significant factors in opening up new international markets. The time of the market entry determines one's own market position and thus the economic success in a new foreign market, too. It impacts one's own internationalization strategy and, via the economies of scope, the entire company. This applies particularly to a transnational organization.

There are various aspects to timing strategies. The first aspect concerns the appropriate time for the company to internationalize. Should it establish a strong market position in the home country first or should it internationalize shortly after being founded? This certainly depends on the corporate vision, the mentality of the owners, the resources available, the business model and the industry. After that a decision has to be taken whether new foreign markets are to be developed parallel to each other or in sequence and whether a company is striving for the role of pioneer or follower.

Timing strategies are competitive strategies. Moreover, they are always a reaction to the actual and expected behavior of competitors. A typical example is the pioneer strategy with which many SMEs try to position themselves as "first movers" by entering a number of foreign markets simultaneously (market penetration strategy). In the process they mainly use market entry forms that are characterized by low resource requirements (for example: licensing).

Parallel or Sequential Developing of new markets

Developing foreign markets occurs parallel or in sequence depending on the industry and one's own company. Usually, companies use a combination of both courses of action.

Sprinkler or Market Penetration Strategy

The company uses the sprinkler or market penetration strategy to enter several foreign markets at the same time or in quick succession. The individual foreign markets can be independent of each other or part of a free-trade area (for example: NAFTA, the EU) or of a geographical region (for example: Scandinavia, the Middle East). The second approach is also referred to as regional market penetration strategy.

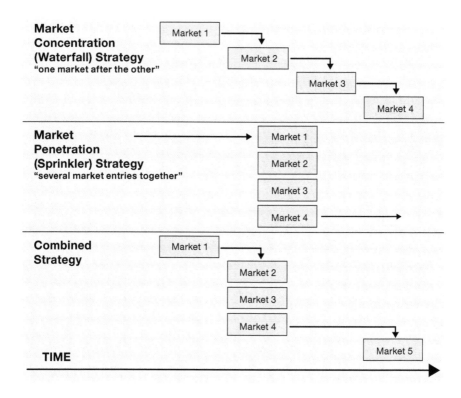

Fig. 12: Parallel and sequential developing of new markets

The market penetration strategy is particularly appropriate for foreign markets with high cultural, geographic and structural proximity (for example: a free-trade area) that stand out by dint of their low market entry barriers and the fact that products and services only require slight adaptation. These prerequisites apply primarily to the two strategies "Global Exporter" and "Born Global" where for competitive reasons establishing a global market position swiftly is crucial.

Apart from the argument in favor of a higher market entry speed (keyword: "time to market") there are advantages in diversifying the market entry risk over a larger number of markets and distributing the administration costs over (it is to be hoped perceptibly) higher sales. Under certain circumstances further synergies and economies of scale arise. The greatest disadvantage is that the market penetration strategy places considerable demands on resources and co-ordination.

Due to inadequate financial and HR resources, a lack of entrepreneurial far sightedness and insufficient qualifications many companies break off their market penetration strategy after the first setbacks. The resulting "internationalization ruins" are not depreciated or renovated which calls into doubt the previous investments and also the entire internationalization strategy.

Waterfall or Market Concentration Strategy

In the waterfall or market concentration strategy a company always concentrates its (limited) resources on the simultaneous entry into one or a small number of foreign markets. As soon as market entry (with the market entry process "*company2newmarket*"; see Chapter 2) has been carried out successfully, the freed-up resources are invested in a new market entry project.

The waterfall or market concentration strategy is particularly appropriate for large, complex and fast growing foreign markets (for example: the USA, China) because market entry requires a substantial use of resources. Companies with limited resources choose this strategy especially for growth markets with the greatest market potential. The gradual internationalization goes easy on resources and permits companies to transfer their experiences to date into new market entry projects.

Combinations of Sprinkler and Waterfall Strategies

In practice, combinations of market penetration and market concentration strategies are used quite often. Regional market penetration strategies are popular in free-trade areas. Thus foreign industrial companies like to enter the Mexican market with one production and sell their products throughout the NAFTA region. In doing so they benefit from low production costs and a large internal market that has considerable purchasing power. Moreover, Mexico has a considerable number of free-trade agreements with third countries which affords further strategic courses of action. A further example of a combination of various timing strategies is market entry into the EU via countries like Ireland or Great Britain. In this case US companies in particular benefit from the cultural and language proximity and ensure market entry from there into the EU.

In both examples various market entry forms are employed. Whereas market entry into Mexico and Ireland /Great Britain usually entails a combination of subsidiary/market concentration strategies, companies usually decide in favor of exports for their market penetration strategy as a market entry form into the NAFTA region and the EU. This way, companies use more resources for market entry into foreign markets that have a high degree of market attractiveness.

Pioneer and Follower Strategies

As timing strategies pioneer and follower strategies are also competitive strategies. A distinction can be made in the latter between so-called early and late followers. At the same time, the internationalization of young companies in particular takes place much earlier today in order to generate pioneer profits and economies of scale.

"First-Mover" or Pioneer Strategies

The traditional pioneer is the company, which is first to enter a foreign market with its products and services. The aim of a pioneer strategy is to develop a market according to one's own ideas and to realize a sustainable competitive advantage in the form of higher profit margins (occasionally first mover profits). This strategy entails implementing product standards and creating brand preferences in customers and their commitment to one's own company. For this purpose a pioneer needs resources, knowledge of the market, and above all excellent contacts to decision-makers. Effective market entry barriers are set up by integrating suppliers and distribution channels, too. Well-known examples of the successful implementation of pioneer strategies are McDonalds in Russia, Volkswagen in China and the Vienna Insurance Group from Austria, which has become the regional market leader due to its market entry into the foreign markets of Central and Eastern Europe and has realized permanently higher returns.

Pioneer strategies are only appropriate for companies that are flexible and dynamic and have a clear vision; that are prepared to accept the financial and in particular the culturally volatile business results and setbacks of their foreign subsidiaries without immediately calling their internationalization strategy into question. Companies need to decide and act quickly if they want to be a "first mover" or pioneer because the so-called "window of opportunity" closes very swiftly again. A great deal of experience in recognizing and implementing market opportunities is required. Today, early warning systems such as the *IMM International*

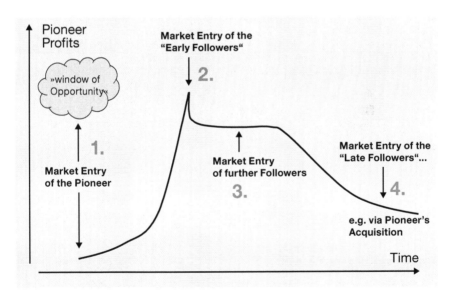

Fig. 13: Developing pioneer profits subject to followers entering the market

Market Monitor are a help. Moreover, it is simply not enough to enter a foreign market early. Instead, the pioneer also needs to be in a position to translate his time advantage into a pioneer profit and competitive advantage before the other competitors catch up. In fact, a pioneer can find it lucrative to sell his company to a "late follower". It can be an attractive opportunity for young, successful entrepreneurs in a foreign market to obtain a high purchasing price.

The disadvantages of the pioneer strategy are to be found in the higher costs of market entry and especially the risks that this entails. Apart from developing the market the pioneer has to continually defend his position against competitors, especially in attractive markets. He has to make use of "opinion leaders" and "early adopters" to generate high profit margins in order to finance the cost of capital and further investments in market growth, innovation and niche products. Therefore, occupying niches and implementing the cost leadership strategy constitute the ideal starting point for the so-called "early followers".

Advantages of pioneer strategies	Advantages of follower strategies
• Generating pioneer profits • Developing the market (products, preferences, brands, IT systems) • Retaining customers, suppliers and distribution channels • Establishing market entry barriers • Occupying the major market positions • Access to infrastructure and scarce resources • Achieving market leadership • Networking within the country and integration into society	• Utilizing existing infrastructure • Fully developed market regulation • Learning from the pioneer's errors • Lower risks and costs, and less time required for market entry • Fewer investments in technologies by copying the market leader • Availability of qualified employees • Existence of suppliers and distribution • Attractive strategic options ranging from niche to cost leadership strategies • Existence of candidates for acquisition

Table 3: Pioneer strategies versus follower strategies

"Follower" Strategies

The "fast/early followers" follow the pioneer directly. From the very beginning they try to benefit from the pioneer's experiences and ground work. This lowers the costs and risks of their market entry and increases its speed. At the same time, they will try to differentiate by taking on the role of the cost leader; by copying the successful products and services of the market leader and offering them at a lower price; and by occupying the remaining market niches. With lower market entry costs and high economies of scale they will try to persevere in their role of cost leader as long as possible.

The "late followers" leave developing the market entirely to their competitors. A foreign market does not become attractive until a certain stage of development has been reached. The criteria for this are among other things the existence of the requisite infrastructure, political stability, a fully operational market and professionally operating suppliers. As soon as these criteria have been met, they try to enter the market by acquiring an appropriate market participant in order to overcome the prevailing barriers to market entry. Such an acquisition is capital intensive because the seller expects his investment to be reimbursed and in addition he expects to receive returns commensurate with the risk involved. This strategy is particularly appropriate for financially sound companies who have experience in integrating acquisitions and enhancing synergy effects.

Competitive Strategies

Pioneer and follower strategies are competitive strategies because they represent a reaction to the actual and expected actions by competitors. Choosing a competitive strategy depends on one's own competitive position, the resources available and the corporate objectives.

Pioneers and/or market leaders have the most difficult market position. They need to keep a constant eye on their competitors and they have to try to maintain their market position. As a result, they strive to increase the volume of the entire market, especially in new foreign markets, because they can benefit best from this. At the same time they defend their market share by establishing or even expanding barriers to market entry.

The competitive strategies of all the competitors are reactions to the activities of the market leader and pioneer from whom they can set themselves apart via cost leadership, product differentiation or by concentrating on certain customer segments. In addition competitors have the opportunity to compete directly or indirectly with the market leader

Niche strategies	Follower strategies	Challenger strategies	Pioneer/market leader strategies
Individual or several market niches according to various criteria such as costs, service, price or customer segments	• Fast/early follower • Slow/late follower	Direct or indirect competition with the market leader / pioneer	• Market growth strategy • Defending market share • Developing market share

Table 4: Competitive and timing strategies

or one of his challengers, or to follow him more quickly or more slowly (for example in respect of new products and services).

Choosing an Appropriate Time for Internationalization

Today, companies internationalize with ever increasing speed and thoroughness. Whereas it used to be that market leadership in the home market was the initial aim, SMEs nowadays produce abroad or export their products to remote growth markets. This trend could first be observed among companies from small home markets. It was solely because of the limited size of their sales markets that they were soon forced to look for customers beyond the borders of their own countries.

There has also been a perceptible increase in the speed of internationalization. At one time, it took almost two generations of global managers to develop a local company into a multi-national company, but today internationalization takes place within a few years, as can be observed in the example of the social media. This also applies to new products that today are launched on the market if not immediately globally (for example: cinema films, smart phones, computer, video games, television, fashion collections, cars) at least simultaneously in a number of countries and with increasingly shorter product lifecycles.

A swift market entry globally makes sense if the industry exhibits considerable advantages for first-movers/pioneers – for example in the field of technology and marketing. These industries (for example: social media) operate according to the principle of "Winner-takes-all". The benefit for the individual member rises with the total number of members.

After investments have been made in the platform (for example: trading and payment systems by Amazon and Ebay) the operator only has quite modest costs for the maintenance and the introduction of further auxiliary services as well as for customer support. The cost of market entry into new foreign markets is mainly restricted to the cost of translation into the respective languages because there are hardly any barriers to market entry. The acquisition of new members is the most expensive item of a global scale model. According to the principle of "Winner-takes-all", the company that can acquire and retain the largest number of members wins the competition.

The social media are an excellent example of this. Following on from the first social networks like Facebook, LinkedIn and Xing new providers established themselves in an increasing number of and in ever smaller niches. Well-known examples are the professional social networks that today offer products for almost every target group and every stage of a career. LinkedIn has caught on worldwide in the meantime whereas Xing focuses on the German–speaking regions. This also applies to social networks for finding a dream partner where meanwhile almost any wish expressed by any target group whether globally or regionally can be fulfilled.

Today, the network concept is also crucial in the internationalization of local companies. Thus freelancers such as graphic designers, advertising agencies, doctors, editors or tax consultants can offer their services at least on a national market and in many cases, like IT experts, on the global market. Manufacturing companies place growing emphasis on their own web shops for their exports. There they can market their products globally above and beyond their existing distribution organization.

Frequently, faster globalization can also be observed in highly concentrated (oligopolistic), stagnating markets (for example: telecommunications, energy, car-makers). Apart from the usual well-known reasons for internationalization, competition is also a strong motive for moving abroad. Individual competitors observe each other critically and fear that a competitor moving abroad could have a negative impact on their own market position. This can lead to market entries that are hard to understand and that are not based on economic criteria.

Technology is the driver in this increasing internationalization. Today, worldwide communication via the Internet – we can use it to phone, we can make video calls or send emails – is almost free of charge. In recent years, there has likewise been a significant drop in the cost of travel and transportation. Mobility has increased. Education, too, is becoming increasingly global. Although most trade and management still take place locally or regionally at most, there is practically no way to stop the process of change.

Choosing the right timing strategy is complex and a great challenge to a global manager. Apart from the actual and expected behavior of competitors, technological development and the opportunities in the various foreign markets, the scope for decision-making with respect to choosing the right timing strategy is defined first and foremost by one's own corporate strategy and the resources available.

Timing strategies are also competitive strategies. They always trigger a reaction from a competitor. Thus entry into a competitor's attractive market can lead to a comparable counter-reaction in an attractive market of one's own. Moreover, market reactions can have very different impacts. Thus a market entry by a late follower can lead to a market exit by competitors, but it can also lead to a huge defense reaction. In the first instance, market objectives will be achieved in all likelihood. In the second instance, the foreign market can, in the long term, lose its attractiveness for all the competitors due to fierce price competition.

Summary

This chapter is a synthesis of the current trends in developing internationalization strategies from the point of view of a practitioner. In the process, the most important elements have been described briefly and their advantages and limitations stated. International companies operate in a dynamic environment where the only reliable constant is permanent change. This places extremely high demands on the corporate vision and on strategies. In addition to the greatest predictability and reliability, an international company requires the flexibility necessary to establish trust, global brands and an excellent reputation in the long term. This poses considerable challenges with respect to the right timing.

Today, the core task of a global manager is establishing competences, networks and interfaces for all internal and external stakeholders. In addition, there is the symbiotic and synergetic union of extremes in various cultures or between global integration and local adaptation. These are the preconditions for all the elements of a transnational organization to function efficiently.

There are no such things as global people and global cultures. People and cultures vary; they are neither better nor worse than others; they are simply different. There are, therefore, limitations to global products and global, universalistic theories. Diversity is the basis for a geocentric perspective and a good starting point for an excellent competitive position.

The chapters that follow will address the most important elements of global market strategy. These are, for example, selecting and assessing foreign markets, choosing the right market entry strategy and dealing with other cultures. They include the market penetration process "*company2new-market*", with which new customers in new foreign markets can be won in less time, with fewer risks and with the use of fewer resources.

Lessons to be learned

1. *Proceed in a structured way*: Begin with your international corporate vision before developing the individual strategic elements!
2. *Utilize all the advantages of global organizations*: Only the transnational organizational structure described here permits an efficient search for and use of competitive advantages.
3. *Think in terms of global networks*: Today, states, companies and people, too, are networking more and more.
4. *Use the opportunities afforded by diversity*: Today, global companies use the advantages of various foreign markets and live this diversity in all divisions of the company.
5. *There are no such things as global cultures and people*: Always adapt your products to your customers. Global products have tended to be global failures.
6. *Unite apparent extremes*: Learn to develop symbioses and synergies from apparent extremes in cultures, partners in joint-ventures and local and global points of view.

7. *Watch out for the right timing*: Do not internationalize when you are ready but when the market is.

8. *Sow growth options*: Options are always opportunities. Invest in foreign markets with long-term growth potential. Then the seed you sow will sprout and bear fruit in the long term.

9. *Implement competitive strategies with care and skill*: In a foreign market the role of the "fast follower" is usually more successful than that of the pioneer. In the beginning concentrate on lucrative market niches.

10. *Establish a network of expertise*: Your business model with its individual competences needs to be your major competitive advantage. This is difficult to copy.

11. *Internationalize with your strengths*: Never underestimate foreign markets. Never go into new foreign markets without having prepared yourself well in advance; always have the necessary respect and a certain amount of humility.

2. "company2newmarket" – Structured Market Entry Processes for Greater Success in New International Markets

Entering international markets overseas is becoming more and more complex. The increasing multi-polarity of the world, the shift in economic performance towards growth markets and the progressively faster technological and political changes are but a few developments that make it necessary for international market entry to become even more professionalized. Global managers talk openly about such challenges while they are sitting over a glass of wine at the bar of an international hotel chain or in an airport lounge. They complain about the increase in work load due to the impact of the debt crisis in Europe (for example), the changes in the political situation in MENA and the growing regulation and tax burden world-wide.

Unlike the economic press which hails examples of success and even sees market entry in China (for example) as a standard program for cowards, global managers face failures which are becoming the rule rather than the exception. Sales and profits are falling short of targets, foreign branches are being closed at a huge loss and at great expense or joint ventures are being terminated. This news is frightening because the only promising future for most medium and large-sized companies is to be found in developing international markets. The so-called "hidden champions" show that only the successful implementation of strategies by (niche) market leaders can ensure the sustainability of a company; this entails their presence on the major growth markets.

This objective can only be achieved if international market entry develops into a sustainable competitive advantage. A structured market entry process (for example: "*company2newmarket*") is a major factor in helping a company to enter new international markets more swiftly and with fewer resources and risks. Nowadays, only those companies that are in a position to sell their technology and products on all major global markets more successfully than their competitors are able to compete effectively.

This chapter aims at presenting such a market entry process. Part I will explain the concept of such a market entry process and parts II-V will describe the individual steps in detail. These steps involve different tasks that are carried out with specialized tools. Part VI will cover market exits. The ability to exit a foreign market successfully is often neglected but is an important competence of every global manager.

2.1. Market Entry Processes – Fundamentals and Tasks

International market entry processes are always based on the experiences and ideas of the process and project management although the implementation of standardized or even universalistic instruments and theories reach their limits very quickly, particularly in international management. A country and often a region, too, differ perceptibly in speech, culture, history, politics or legislation. Uniting these apparent extremes in the desire for efficiency, local adaptation and for instruments to enable good management in unknown foreign markets is the basis for developing market entry processes.

Every country manager abroad fears the visits by the global manager and his retinue independent of whether it is the export manager, the regional sales manager, the head of a foreign department or even a managing director. They fear the frequently long, useless discussions, irrelevant advice and counter-productive tasks.

How come? Global managers are in charge of a huge number of markets. Usually, their knowledge of their overseas branches is merely superficial and they know even less about the local culture and the idiosyncrasies of the foreign market. In contrast, they are more than familiar with the sensitivities displayed by the central administration towards overseas branches abroad, which is something most managers of branch offices experience in the discussions. Moreover, most companies do not have comparable and meaningful management tools or a powerful management information system. Nevertheless, everyone expects the global manager to make competent and clear decisions.

Global managers love to "export" would-be solutions. If they have found a solution to a problem in one country, they proudly try to implement this in every other market even when this problem does not exist there. This raises a lot of dust, which only settles when the global manager has left to continue his travels (management-by-helicopter). The country manager of the branch office regards the visit as a success if he manages to avoid pointless projects and can address his real problems.

These (unfortunately true) events show that in cases of doubt, your professional experience and even your culture count for little or absolutely nothing abroad; moreover, they cannot count for anything because your own success is based on experiences in a different country with a different culture that cannot necessarily be transferred to other countries. Without appropriate tools to interpret the specific culture, market conditions and the key conditions for success, you are blind.

Therefore, it is advisable to implement a structured market entry process to solve the problem. This consists of management processes and core and support processes; it can be adapted flexibly to the specific corporate strategy and is appropriate for controlling all foreign activities and for individual market entry projects or even market exits. At the same time, it enables the global manager to make more informed decisions on growth and entry into and exit from international markets.

The market entry process "company2newmarket" was devised by the author. It has undergone continual development and has proved to be highly successful in numerous practical trials and university studies. The market entry process "company2newmarket" is based on an active market research based market entry strategy. As a result, a company makes a conscious strategic decision to internationalize and actively begins to select and enter the most attractive foreign markets. A further condition is that a company has a business model that can be "internationalized", knows its strengths and weaknesses as well as its core competences and competitive advantages, and has safeguarded its technologies, products and brands with patents, and its design samples and trademark rights within the framework of an IP strategy. These and other points, too, are recorded in an evaluation of the "international market position" prior to any project and gaps are closed at the customer's request. When the project has reached a successful conclusion, it is awarded a "Fit for International Management" label.

The market entry process *"company2newmarket"* forms the operative bridge between corporate strategy and the planned objectives in international markets. The core process (see Fig. 14) consists of four sub-processes referred to as steps. Each of these four steps comprises various tasks. Each needs to be completed before the next task can be commenced. For this purpose standardized tools are offered that are adapted to the specific requirements of overseas management. At the end of each step there is a milestone where checks are made whether the targets set have been reached and decisions are made whether the next step can now be carried out or whether the project will be abandoned entirely. A market entry project is not completed until all four steps have been carried out in entirety and successfully. This approach affords the project management, the global manager and all decision-makers a transparent overview and the full control of investments and results at all times.

Fig. 14: Market entry process *"company2newmarket"*

The market entry process *"company2newmarket"* contains the following features:

- It is universalistic, which means that it forms a framework for controlling all foreign activities independent of market and industry.

- It can be deployed multi-culturally. That means it can be deployed in both individualistic and in collectivist cultures; it is flexible with regard to its parallel or sequential processing and always integrates both environmental factors and various stakeholders.
- It is performance oriented; it helps to improve the efficiency and effectiveness of all foreign activities in the long term.
- It professionalizes the development and control of new international markets. As a result it is possible to manage more foreign markets simultaneously and successfully.
- It is a learning process that can be adapted flexibly to the current and future requirements of a company. Moreover, it is possible to derive international "best practices" and "benchmarks" that facilitate the exchange between the individual national subsidiaries as well as collaboration in international project groups and the exchange of employees within the framework of international HR development.
- It is specific. Due to the high degree of complexity, every market entry project is broken down into four steps. Each has definite objectives (milestones) that can be achieved by completing clearly defined tasks with efficient and well tried tools. The organization of the project is such that the overview is not lost in the attention to important details.
- It is neutral, which means that the steps, tasks, tools and milestones are transparent, comparable, objective and measurable and can be multiplied.
- It is final. The successful completion of Step 4 marks the end of the market entry project and consequently, the young overseas branch is integrated into the existing management and organization structure.
- It can be multiplied so that several market entry projects can be carried out simultaneously.
- The results of the market entry process "company2newmarket" offer the global manager an objective foundation for decision making on the basis of top-quality data.
- It contains feedbacks, repetitions and the overlapping of tasks because results can change on account of newly acquired knowledge or shifts in the market environment so that decisions taken earlier can stop making sense. Nonetheless, the individual steps, tasks and tools build on one another.

Structured market entry processes help to develop new foreign markets in a more efficient and sustainable manner. They offer companies the advantage of winning new customers in new markets more swiftly and with fewer resources and risks. They provide the global manager with a valuable set of tools for making more informed decisions. Market entry processes are scalable. Their implementation means that more market entry projects can be worked on in parallel and using the same resources. In addition, an enormous amount of knowledge is acquired in developing foreign markets and this is circulated throughout the entire organization.

2.2. Step 1: Market Evaluation and Selection

Selecting foreign markets usually goes beyond any rational line of argument. Over and above the frequently quoted "gut feeling", the location of one's own holiday cottage, language skills, the origin of one's partner or fear of flying and overwork are all put forward, for example, as subjective arguments in favor of the choice of market and such subjective arguments can hardly be refuted. That is not the objective. However, you can be supported by professionally obtained and evaluated facts and arguments as the basis for the decisions to be taken by owners, the board of directors or the management.

The objective of Step 1 "Market Evaluation and Selection" is therefore the selection of the most attractive foreign markets. In the process, foreign markets are chosen where the company in question has the best chances of sustainable success. The results of the evaluations only comprise facts and support preparations for the decision making process. At the same time it can happen that (currently) there is no foreign market that fulfils the criteria stipulated. Thus the objective of Step 1 has not been achieved and the various foreign markets remain under observation over a period of time until a market opportunity arises (or the criteria are adapted). This shows the strength of the modular structure. It is only after the first step has been completed successfully that the steering committee or the management gives the green light for work on the next step.

In practice, a three-step process for market evaluation and selection has asserted itself – from the selection of appropriate foreign markets (Task 1) via the evaluation of market attractiveness (Task 2) to the development of the market penetration strategy (Task 3) – according to the principle: "The more attractive a market is the more it is examined in detail." Using the results of Task 3 it is possible to work out a recommendation for a market entry form (Task 4).

Today, market evaluation and market selection is not only based on national boundaries. An increasing number of companies concentrate on individual regions, towns or target groups in a foreign market or across several countries. In addition, internationalization is gaining ever-greater significance in networks of existing customers and their travel routes. Existing customers are for example delighted to find their favorite brands abroad, which they in turn recommend to local friends, business partners, and hopefully also to local opinion leaders. Furthermore, they will communicate their product preferences to their (social media) network; irrespective of the country in which each individual contact currently lives.

Task 1: Selecting Appropriate Foreign Markets

First of all, the foreign markets that may be appropriate have to be examined. As these can amount to as many as 200, it is important to reduce their number as swiftly as possible. On the one hand, it is important that all the potentially attractive foreign markets are identified i.e. that no attractive foreign market is excluded, and on the other hand, that all the foreign markets that are not attractive (at the moment) are identified as quickly and reliably as possible and are excluded from the selection process immediately. At the end of this task usually 15-25 foreign markets have been selected for further processing.

A selection method which is appropriate and very popular is, for example, the checklist method. By means of clearly defined criteria which are crucial for success, checks are made as to whether a country satisfies these criteria or not. As soon as it has been ascertained that a foreign market has not fulfilled a criterion, it is excluded from any further processing.

Internal variables or one's own strategic requirements are recommended as criteria. At the same time, internal criteria such as resources and competences or external market criteria such as the existence of double taxation agreements and free-trade agreements or qualified employees can be adopted, too. In principle, the information should be easy to collect and be available in excellent data quality.

Before carrying out the checklist, it is important to exclude those countries

- where the company already operates;
- whose values do not correspond to those of the management (rejecting foreign markets for ethical, political or other reasons);
- that do not comply with the specified strategic framework conditions (for example: Triad countries, the European Union or the Growth8 markets);
- that do not satisfy certain maximum and minimum requirements specified by certain criteria as for example a minimum market volume;
- where there are realistic objections such as a lack of (current) demand.

The following example of a medium-sized export-oriented engineering company demonstrates the development of checklist criteria:

- To justify market entry economically the *market potential* has to reach a minimum value which is to be defined.
- The existence of a *free-trade agreement* secures among other things property rights such as patents and protects from expropriation.
- Implementation of the business model is not possible if there are no efficient *institutions* and *infrastructure*.
- The price of products depends among other things on *the exchange rate, import tariffs, and logistics costs.* Excessive costs in any one of these fields are a "killer criterion".
- What are the actual requirements of the customers? Is there any demand at all?

The choice of criteria is very particular. There is an explicit search for so-called "killer criteria" that independent of the results of other criteria make market entry perceptibly difficult. In our example, only Country A fulfils all the criteria.

The data received are transferred into the *"IMM International Market Monitor"*. This is an IMIS (International Market Information System) that provides constantly updated information about numerous foreign

Nr.	Criteria	COUNTRY A	COUNTRY B	COUNTRY C
1	Share of industry in GNP >x % and industrial production >x bn. euro	yes	no	yes
2	Existence of a free-trade agreement	yes	yes	yes
3	Increase in price of currency of target country	yes	yes	no
4	Import tariffs on industrial products <10 %	yes	yes	yes
5	Customers see demand and recognize benefit from use of machinery	yes	no	yes
6	Logistics costs <10 % of entire costs	yes	yes	yes
7	The necessary infrastructure and respective institutions are present	yes	no	no
8...15	...further criteria			

Table 5: Check list for selecting foreign markets

markets. On the one hand, this information can be used for the checklist method within the framework of Task 1 (Selecting Appropriate Foreign Markets) in Step 1 (Market Evaluation and Selection). On the other hand the IMIS is an early warning system which provides information on trends in the various foreign markets. Thus, for example, the attractiveness of a market can increase suddenly due to the conclusion of a free-trade agreement which means that it is then worth considering this foreign market for market entry. On the other hand, deterioration in economic data such as economic stagnation, growing unemployment amongst young people and galloping National Debt, can reduce the attractiveness of the market.

The challenge of an IMIS is in selecting reliable sources and examining the data collected to check whether they are up-to-date, relevant, accurate, complete, reliable, valid and comparable. The list of requirements is long and the challenges are considerable. This begins already with the cultural context. People from other cultures respond to survey questions in different ways no matter how clear these questions may appear to us.

Thus it can happen that questions are answered with absolute conviction in the affirmative out of politeness or to save face even though the person you are talking to may possibly have understood nothing of the topic. Foreign markets with a pronounced bureaucracy often excel at "work arounds". Consequently, the result of your market research will never reflect the actual conditions. Local competitors who have come to terms with the framework conditions may well be very profitable even though this is scarcely understandable when regarded from the outside. Therefore, it is important to take the cultural context into consideration when asking questions and the answers need to be confirmed by at least a second source.

Task 2: Calculating Market Attractiveness

The remaining 15–25 foreign markets are subject to detailed analysis according to the motto: the more attractive a foreign market is the more it is subject to an intensive analysis. In principle the fields to be analyzed can be divided into four criteria: framework conditions and country

	Specification of criteria	Evaluation country A	Evaluation country B	Weighting factors	Result country A	Result country B
Political risks	Country risk	high (= 3)	low (=1)	2	6	2
Regulation	Authorization	medium (=2)	medium	3	6	6
Economic structure / institutions	Control and legal system	high	low	3	9	3
Social and cultural structures	Cultural distance	medium	medium	2	4	4
Geographical and climatic factors	Climate	high	high	1	3	3
Result of field analyzed	Additional factors	–	–	–	28	18

Table 6: Framework conditions and country risks

risks, industry-specific market potential, competitive strength and one's own competitive position (in the new foreign market). Each field to be examined has between five and ten criteria, which are partly identical with the *IMM International Market Monitor* but in this case they are analyzed and scrutinized in depth. The data of the individual criteria are collected and evaluated (for example: scoring model). Moreover, it is possible to supplement with additional weighting factors.

Table 6 shows the implementation of a simple scoring model. Each evaluation criterion has further sub-criteria which have not been presented here.

The following criteria are recommended as further fields to be analyzed:

- Industry-specific market potential
- Market volume
- Market growth
- Customer structure
- Price ranges
- Market access
- Intensity of competition
- Market significance of competitors
- Origin and structure
- Cost structures
- Performance strategies
- Output capacities
- Distribution, communication, prices and service
- Own competitive position
- Market suitability of one's own services and product portfolio
- Business potential
- Availability of resources
- Relative competitive advantages
- Protection of intellectual property

In this analysis, barriers to both market entry and exit are crucial factors. Even if the latter appears to be a little premature, it is very important to know – against the background of constant political changes – how to get out of a country again before you enter it. In this respect a barrier to a market exit is at the same time a barrier to a market entry. On the one hand, barriers to market exits contain emotional elements such as loyalty to a country and people or a loss of image; on the other hand, they contain economic elements such as state restrictions and interdependency, high handling costs, depreciation for enterprise value and repayments of subsidies. In industries with considerable barriers to market exit (for example: the automotive industry) a market entry can lead to overcapacities which are difficult to reduce and which lower the profits of all market participants as long as they continue.

Traditional barriers to market entry are economies of scale and economies of scope, cost and competitive advantages in the form of product differentiation such as brand preference, and access to distribution channels. Likewise, competitors' behavior can also be barriers to market entry. This includes among other things threats of retaliation, price decreases (marginal price strategy) or customer retention with a view to increasing switching costs. In addition there are one's own costs for winning new customers. State barriers to market entry such as subsidies and authorizations can work in both directions. State agencies, therefore, look for international investors in almost every country; this is referred to as location marketing. On the other hand, states restrict companies in their scope of action as can be seen in the example of China, that, for instance, requires companies in certain industries to form joint ventures with local partners, to produce in the country itself ("local content" regulations) or to hand on technologies. Most barriers to market entry evolve from consumer and environmental laws and are the minimum statutory demands on companies, their products and employees' qualifications, which differ from one country to another.

The existing institutions and the prevailing infrastructure of a foreign market are a further criterion. In highly specialized national economies companies often concentrate only on a small part of the supply chain. In other foreign markets there is a frequent lack of providers of certain products and services. This needs to be taken into consideration in developing the business model in step 2 (Market Preparation) because, if necessary, further competences will need to be added in compensation. Transactions provide a good example of this. If insurance companies or fund providers wish to offer savings schemes with monthly payments in an attractive target market, they are dependent on an inexpensive and highly efficient transaction system. Every false entry and every return impact the administration costs of this one customer immediately. For this reason, the company has the choice of establishing a transaction system on its own, finding another company to do it or not working the market. Consequently, an evaluation of market attractiveness also entails questions on the lack of market institutions, the impact on one's one business model and avenues for compensation.

After data has been collected and evaluated in all four fields, it can been summarized as shown in Table 7:

Fields to be analyzed	Country A	Country B	Country C	Country D	Country E
Framework conditions and country risks	28	18	32	13	23
Industry specific market potential	8	33	29	17	17
Intensity of Competition	12	34	25	21	18
Own competitive position	26	25	31	29	28
Result	74	110	117	80	86

Table 7: Evaluation of a foreign market analysis

This evaluation creates a ranking list of all the foreign markets analyzed for their market attractiveness. Usually four or five foreign markets are suitable for further analysis. In our case these would be countries B and C, whereby the field "Framework conditions and country risks" of country B ought to be subjected to very thorough scrutiny again.

Many emerging growth markets are characterized by a high industry-specific market potential, a low overall intensity of competition, and the strong competitive position of the company willing to enter the market. In contrast, the infrastructure is still weak and the political risk is high in comparison to developed markets. Consequently, opportunities for greater growth and higher returns usually also mean higher risks and vice versa.

Basically, such a method can be regarded very critically because the choice of criteria, their evaluation and rating, for example, can be termed discretionary due to the global manager's personal background and the selection of company-specific criteria. In this connection the sentence comes to mind very quickly: "Don't trust any statistics that you haven't prepared yourself."

Nevertheless, I would recommend implementing such a method. On the one hand, it forces a global manager to have a serious look at and collect information on the markets and to set up a network of contacts. On the other hand, my own experience shows that the results are not so far apart even if various groups often evaluate and rate various criteria differently. The prerequisite is of course that implementation has to be both professional and unbiased.

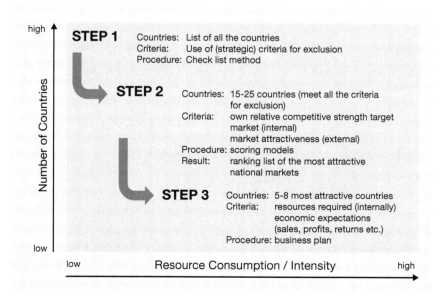

Fig. 15: Three-step market evaluation and selection process

Task 3: Selecting a Market Entry Form

A market entry form is chosen according to its market attractiveness; one's own competitive strengths and the cultural distance between the home land and the target market (see Fig. 16). The selection is based on the assumption that a company can take greater risks as competitive strength and market attractiveness increase. Selecting the market entry form also forms the basis of the market selection in Task 4.

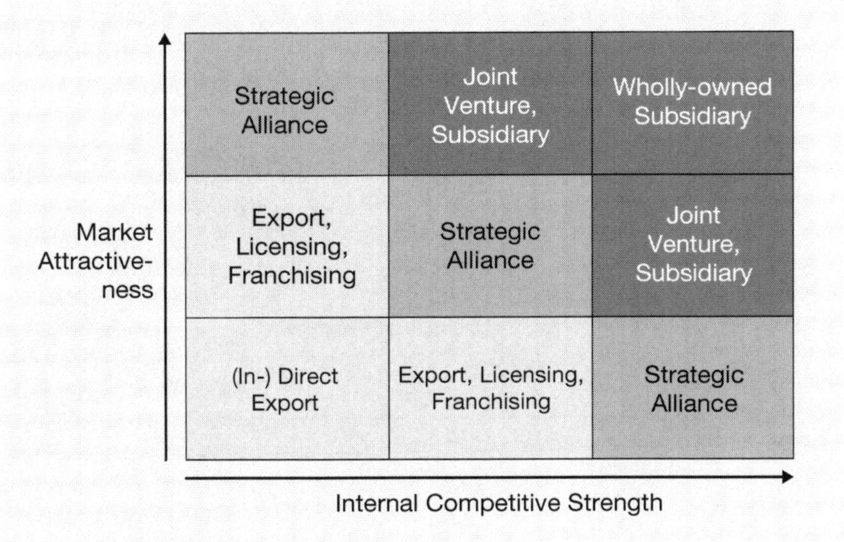

Market Attractive-ness	Strategic Alliance	Joint Venture, Subsidiary	Wholly-owned Subsidiary
	Export, Licensing, Franchising	Strategic Alliance	Joint Venture, Subsidiary
	(In-) Direct Export	Export, Licensing, Franchising	Strategic Alliance

Internal Competitive Strength

Fig. 16: Market attractiveness portfolio with recommendation for market entry forms

The form chosen here is the first step in the market entry process. For that reason it is always advisable – as far as possible in the industry – to select a market entry form like exports, for example, which only entails slight risks. As market success and knowledge increase, the market entry form can become riskier and use more resources. After the export phase, a sales office could be opened which would gradually take over further tasks such as warehousing, assembly, repairs and applied research. In a final step a competitor could be acquired or a factory of one's own could be built. This procedure is also referred to as the phase model of market entry (see Step 4).

If there is a high cultural distance, it is advisable to look for support from or collaboration with local partners who help to bridge the cultural differences (see Fig. 17). Market entry forms with local partners are for example licensing, franchising, strategic alliances or joint ventures. Current research shows, however, that companies tend to choose their own branch office as a market entry form despite the advantages afforded by a partnership. The disadvantages of being dependent on a local partner seem to outweigh the advantages. Further reasons are the frequent failure of joint ventures and the outflow of knowledge to future competitors. However, the partner in a joint venture can assume the market entry risks and in Step 4 (Market Growth) sell out to the global manager. This lowers the market entry costs and risks for the global manager considerably.

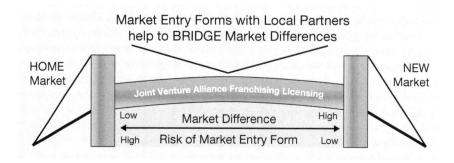

Fig. 17: Partnerships to bridge cultural, geographical and political/legal differences

The selection of a market entry form is therefore based on the company, its industry and the corporate strategy:

- Financial service providers such as banks, for example, are the most regulated industry. They actually have only two market entry forms open to them: "buy" (acquisition) or "build" (subsidiary), because they require authorization to operate prior to commencing operations and are subject to regular checks afterwards. To evaluate the market they can open a representative office that is not allowed to engage in any economic activities, however. This barrier to market entry increases market entry costs and the length of the project significantly and seriously restricts the various courses of action in the business model. As a result, an inefficient market emerges that means high costs for the customers on account of bureaucracy and partitioning. Should a company achieve sustainable success with its market entry, it is protected just like the other local participants are and benefits from the considerable barriers to market entry.
- Fast-Food-Restaurants have perceptibly greater freedom selecting a market entry form. As a result McDonald's works almost entirely with two market entry forms – franchising and their own restaurants. In contrast, Starbucks uses, in addition to their own cafés, licensing (in

the entire country) and joint ventures as market entry forms. The latter is to bridge the cultural distance between the business model and the taste and behavior of customers in the target market. Moreover, local partners such as the Tata Group in India might have access to the best retail locations, which are essential for the success of retailers like H & M or Inditex.

Task 4: Market Selection

Global managers begin to select a market on the basis of the ranking list of target markets ranged according to market attractiveness, the market attractiveness portfolio (see Fig. 18) and the market entry form chosen in Task 3. It is here that they concentrate on the foreign markets E, F and H. In the case of these three foreign markets they expect to be able to operate successfully with the resources and competences on hand.

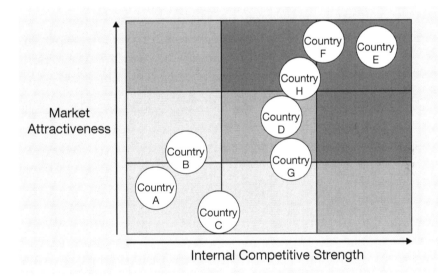

Fig. 18: Market attractiveness portfolio with positioning of the foreign markets analyzed

This selection process is supplemented and underpinned by a preliminary rudimentary business plan (see also Step 2 Task 5), which presents the very different economic effects of the selection. At this stage the business plan is still based largely on suppositions which, in the course of the market entry process *"company2newmarket"*, can be replaced with concrete knowledge and the results obtained. Only the budget for Step 2 is presented in detail for every potential foreign market and includes all the objectives, activities, costs and the time required.

For this purpose, further assumptions are made. These are, among other things, the market segments dealt with in the first step and the products offered, prices, distribution channels, locations and logistics. These points just like the penetration or absorption strategy are part of the strategy profile which is likewise created in Step 2.

Drawing up a business plan at this point can certainly be open to the criticism that it is much too early. This is all the more understandable as no project plan or an extensive feasibility study has been drawn up. However, experience shows that there are always questions about costs as soon as a decision has to be taken. Therefore, global managers need to be able to answer questions about what the next step will cost and what results they expect from this market entry project. The right tool is a sophisticated business plan, which includes among others a project-, investment- and cash flow plan and is based on the corporate reporting tools. The first data are based on assumptions from earlier market entry projects and on the market data available from the *IMM International Market Monitor*.

The aim of Step 1 "Market Evaluation and Selection" is to identify appropriate foreign markets. In a three-step method the most attractive foreign markets are selected, their market attractiveness calculated and presented in a ranking list and portfolio, a market entry form is selected and a preliminary business plan drawn up. Thus the decision-makers have detailed information on hand to help them to decide to grant approval for Step 2.

Although the cost of Step 1 is still relatively clear, it is advisable to set up or acquire a reliable market information system like the *IMM International Market Monitor*. This system stores the market research results that are required in the steps that follow. This means that comparable projects can be implemented at considerably less expense in future. Moreover, the market information system also serves as an early warning instrument for external opportunities and risks.

In the project, the cost of Step 1 "Market Evaluation and Selection" remains within reasonable limits. The decision to prepare market entry for one or two foreign markets in Step 2 means that costs will increase perceptibly and (at least internally) the awareness of the project increases in the company due to the involvement of a growing number of employees. Consequently the quality of the results in Step 1 is crucial for all further steps.

2.3. Step 2: Market Preparation

After the decision by the management to implement Step 2 for one or several foreign markets, a market entry project begins for one specific foreign market. As a result, every company faces an increase in risks and costs which can, however, be calculated at any time due to the structured approach.

The major task in this step is selecting the project team, especially the local executives. The quality of each member of the project staff is crucial for the success of any market entry project. Consequently, global managers will only continue with further tasks if they are absolutely convinced that they have the right team and particularly that the key positions have been filled with the very best.

The aim of Step 2 – to draw up a business plan with a practicable business model for a (still) unknown foreign market – is a huge challenge to all the project staff. However, they have a number of efficient tools that have also been tried and tested in other international projects to help them cope. In this case the key management task of global managers is developing and training the team in the application of these tools. As far as the tasks are concerned, the quality of the results is to the fore because, in the steps that follow, it is almost impossible to rectify any errors made at this stage. The project staff will place their hopes on existing competitive advantages and their most attractive products and services in order to increase the likelihood of success.

Task 1: Establishing a Project Organization and Selecting the Project Team

Choosing the right employees is crucial for the success of a market entry project. It is the global manager's responsibility to integrate the members of the team with their various cultural backgrounds and usually from various locations into one organization. The selection of the organization form is based on the internationalization strategy whereby particular emphasis is placed on collaboration, communication and decision-making.

Selecting the Project Team

People make the difference. The quality of the project staff is decisive for the success of the project. From my own experience, I can only advise every global manager and project manager not to take up work on the project before they have selected a team comprised of experienced professionals. This applies both to selecting expatriates and selecting local executives.

Expatriates provide experience of various market entry projects and know the company with its resources, competences and competitive advantages. This is extremely valuable in every phase of the project. If, for example, market entry in Step 3 does not work as planned, they can fall back on the company's fund of knowledge and solutions in other foreign markets. However, they are also aware of the fact that the success of the project depends ultimately on the local employees. The market entry project will only succeed if the local culture is integrated and the local employees are prepared for the task of taking over the management eventually.

Acquiring good employees in new markets is a challenge. This applies to the General Manager in particular. Most successful local executives avoid the risks, the effort and a start-up with which they are scarcely familiar. If it fails, an international company leaves the country but the General Manager who fails remains. This fear is easy to understand. Thus the only alternative that often remains is to establish a General Manager who comes from lower in the hierarchy and who will grow with the company. He ought to understand this step in his career as an opportunity and have considerable potential for development. Especially in the beginning, key factors are, therefore, thinking and acting in terms of the company, intercultural competence and language skills, experience in international companies and contacts to the foreign market.

Regrettably, this advice is not taken to heart even though managements know better. Today, selecting the wrong employee is the rule rather than the exception. It is not unusual that two or three local General Managers have been appointed before the market entry process "*company2newmarket*" has been completed. Consequently, many global managers act as General Managers in a part-time capacity because high fluctuation among local General Managers tends to be the norm. This approach means that they very quickly reach the limits of their ability to withstand stress and the entire internationalization strategy is in danger of failing. In practice I have seen this happening more than once.

Setting up the Project Organization

The project staff fall back on the resources of the staff department "*New Market Development*" (see Fig. 19). Here competences in the field of international HR management, project management (Project Office) und international market research are in place. This also includes knowledge of the business model of the individual subsidiaries in the foreign markets and the specific competences of new and former project staff and expatriates. Thus a *virtual network organization* arises in which experts are used where they are most needed.

Fig. 19: Support functions in the field of new markets

As the project organization itself is very similar to that of a traditional project, it will not be amplified any further. However, it does differ in two main aspects. On the one hand, the project organization gradually develops into a corporate organization in the course of the market entry

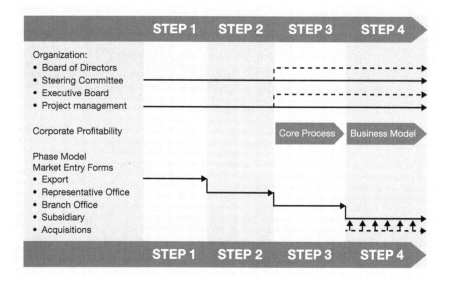

Fig. 20: Organization development during the four steps of the market entry process *"company2newmarket"*

process *"company2newmarket"* (see Fig. 20). As soon as a branch office exists, the corporate boards are filled with the respective project managers. This creates continuity.

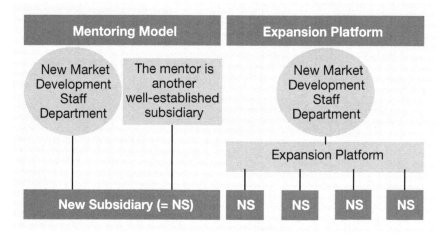

Fig. 21: Mentoring models and platform models as examples of-organization forms of market entry projects

On the other hand, various models such as the *Mentoring Model* and the *Expansion Platform* (see Fig. 21) are used, depending on the market entry strategy. The former is used for *market concentration strategy* and the latter is used for *market penetration strategy*. As a result, an entire free-trade area or a region of similar foreign markets with a small CAGE (cultural, administrative, geographical and economic) distance is developed by using the *Expansion Platform*. The *Mentoring Model* is used mainly to enter a single foreign market.

Task 2: Developing the Market Position

The project team's first task is to specify the market position. Specifying the product portfolio and defining the customer segment to be targeted are to the fore whereby the project team will select products, which afford the company the greatest competitive advantage.

Market Research

Developing the market position is based on comprehensive market research (see Fig. 22). The quality of the results depends on the quality of the cultural coding. This includes, among other things, how questions are posed and how the answers are interpreted. In many cultures direct questions can lead to wrong answers. The persons interviewed wish to save face and prefer to give a wrong answer rather than admit that there is a gap in their knowledge. Thus the results of the market research are, at best, distorted. Actually they are worthless. They are also referred to as "garbage-in, garbage-out". It is also important to choose the right interview partner. Is the expert really so respected? Does the composition of experts in the random sample really cover every aspect?

It is here that global managers need to be at the forefront of developments and to make use of professional support. Only in talks with opinion leaders, experts, partner companies and competitors can they get a feel for the market. These talks are unstructured. As questions are open, individual themes can be addressed in detail. The aim of these initial talks is to prepare for the second round of the market research and these result in the first rudimentary positioning alternatives.

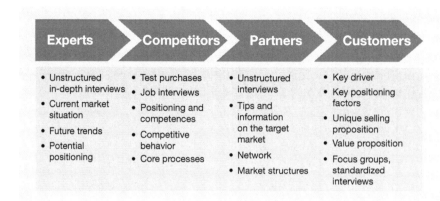

Fig. 22: Target groups and techniques for market research in new foreign markets.

The results are now presented to potential customers in focus groups where they are discussed and optimized. As a rule, two or three rounds are needed until a useable result is obtained. Usually this contains at least two or three positioning alternatives that will then be tested in a representative survey. The market research is concluded when this survey has been evaluated.

Market Positioning

The first result of the market research is the key-driver analysis. A key driver is a feature of a product or service that is a key factor in the customer's decision to purchase. As different customers prefer different features, there are usually several key drivers. An additional benefit that is not crucial in the purchasing decision but that can have a favorable impact on the price-performance ratio is referred to as value added. Another important factor that needs to be taken into account is the entry ticket. These are features of a product or service that do not influence the decision to purchase but have to be satisfied at all costs. An example of this is the error-free payment by credit card.

Tip: It is worth developing the product in conjunction with test customers. That way you obtain a marketable product, initial references and the first revenues. If the test customer is also one of your best cus-

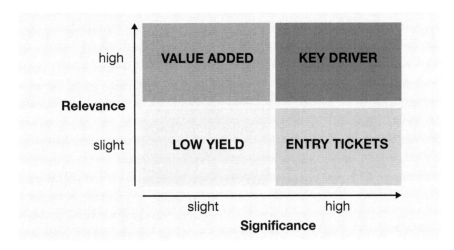

Fig. 23: Key-driver analysis

tomers, as is often the case in the B2B business of suppliers, it is unlikely that anything can go wrong.

The key features of the product for the positioning of the product in the target market and for setting it apart from the competition are compiled from the key-driver analysis. This is also referred to as USP (unique selling proposition). This positioning differs in some points from market to market but the product is not modified radically. It merely means that in other cultures other features of the same product or features that have been added are crucial for purchasing. Thus, in many countries an automatic gearbox in a new car is the requisite for the decision to purchase (entry ticket) whereas in other countries it is merely an option (value added).

The benefits promised to the customer or the features of the product are referred to as value proposition. The global manager should also take care that the positioning is sustainable and that the appropriate competence and competitive advantages are in place. It can be seen from the current IP battle between international electronic companies that a company's competitive advantages are defended tooth and nail and protected because it is they alone that can secure sustainable growth.

Strategy Profile

The global manager can now draw up a strategy profile. A modified An-soff-Matrix (see Fig. 24) can help to develop strategic alternatives with regards to the choice of products and services, customer segments and foreign markets. In this connection the question is paramount: Which (existing, modified or new) products are to be sold to which target groups, at which locations (for example: metropolises first of all) and via which distribution channels in the new foreign market?

The answer is recorded in a strategy profile, which consists of the ba-sis- and strategy style as well as the strategy substance and strategy field. The basis style describes the degree of standardization or the degree of adaptation of the product to the requirements of the target market; strat-egy style describes the approach to competitors; the strategy substance describes the customer benefits and the strategy field is the target group to be dealt with in respect of market entry.

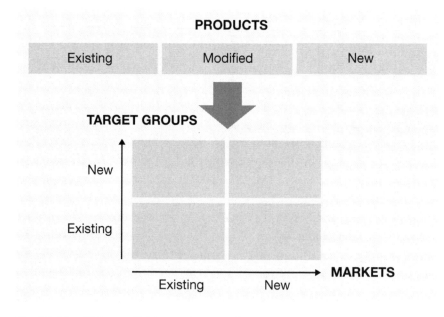

Fig. 24: Identifying suitable products and customer segments

Tactical Profile

The tactical strategy in the market is determined with the aid of the SWOT analysis. It is a powerful tool that is usually not applied consistently enough. First of all, the global manager needs to make a SWOT analysis for each target market because the external perspective with its opportunities and risks varies from country to country. This also applies to the internal perspective. What is strength in one market can be weakness in another market and vice versa. A good example of this is the strength of the market leadership or brand awareness. What is the great strength on the home market rather tends to be a weakness in a new market (see Fig. 25).

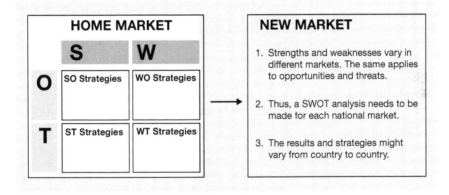

Fig. 25: Developing alternative courses of action with the SWOT analysis

On the basis of the country-specific SWOTs the global manager draws up generic alternative strategies SO (strength opportunities), WO (weakness opportunities), ST (strength threats) and WT (weakness threats). In a second step the connections and causalities between the individual alternative strategies have to be made clear and the following questions answered: Are the existing strengths sufficient for use to be made of the opportunities in the new foreign markets? Are the weaknesses an obstacle to successful market entry?

Tip: Errors in market positioning cannot be rectified in the subsequent tasks and steps. It is advisable for every global manager to invest a great deal of time and effort in obtaining high quality results.

Task 3: Developing the Process Model

Developing the process model is also based on the SPOT concept. The tool is used first of all to draw up the *strategy* and then to draw up the *process model*; then the *organization* is developed and finally decisions are reached on the utilization of essential *technologies*. This means that for example, information and communications systems are adapted to strategy, processes and organization and not vice versa.

In practice there are usually specifications throughout the company that restrict the global manager's freedom to act. Nevertheless, this structured approach has proved effective because this way the scope for action is exploited and the best results obtained.

Taking all Stakeholders into Consideration

Task 2 is mainly concerned with the customers. Moreover, to develop the process model in Task 3 it is essential to have knowledge of one's own competitive situation and especially of the large number of stakeholders in an international environment. Tools such as Porter's "Five Forces Model" are a great help. These can be adapted easily to the requirements

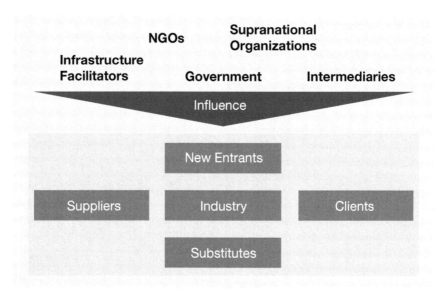

Fig. 26: Adapted Five Forces Model

of global managers who can supplement Porter's model, as necessary, with further forces that are relevant to the foreign market in question (see Fig. 26); for example the existing infrastructure, the government with all the political risks or international NGOs that may be particularly present in that country. The dynamics between the individual forces under the country-specific framework conditions are particularly fascinating. The findings can be used for appropriate competitive strategies. However this means a great deal of work for global managers to start with. They need to ascertain which stakeholders they can integrate into their process model and which mutual dependencies and connections exist.

Activities and Competences

Starting points for differentiating from competitors are to be found in the entire company and not only in products, services and prices. Every company is a network or a combination of various coordinated activities and skills which are essential for implementing the business model. At

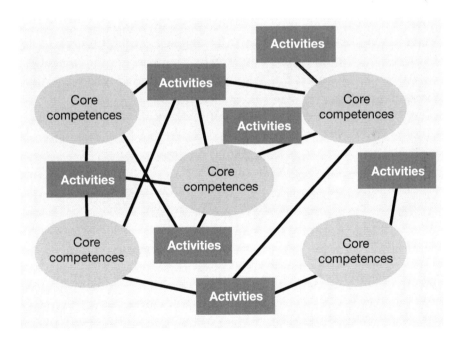

Fig. 27: Network of core competences as a basis for international competitive advantages

best, this network forms a competitive advantage which is difficult to copy. The challenge to competitors is that individual competitive advantages can be copied but it is practically impossible to copy an entire network. Excellent examples of such a resource-based business model are Ryanair, the no-frills airline and ZARA, the fashion producer and trader. To implement their positioning ZARA have established a state of the art, flexible production system, and offer new collections at very frequent intervals.

In this task global managers first of all draw up a list of all the activities in logical sequence and describe which skills are needed for their implementation and whether they do in fact exist. In a second step the connections and dependencies are examined and presented in a network (see Fig. 27).

The so-called process model can now be used as a further tool (see Fig. 28). It represents the practical implementation of the market entry strategy to achieve the goals in the foreign market in question. In addition to the core processes, it also shows management and support processes. An alternative would be other models like Porter's Value Chain.

The use of a process model has proved to be successful in practice because in Step 2 the project team only concentrates on the activities in the core processes and thus on essentials. Furthermore the measuring tools build on the process model and the format is easy for all the project staff and external stakeholders to understand.

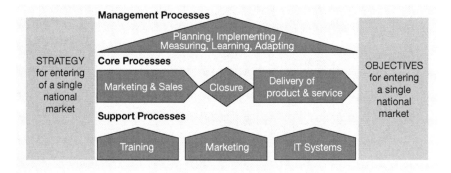

Fig. 28: Basic structure of a process model

Usually, market entry takes place with the most attractive product (or the most attractive range of products) via a distribution channel, so that the core process in developing the market and in providing services, too, is simple and clear in this project phase. Higher demands are made on the management process. In Step 3 "Market Entry", in particular, it is essential that the results are measured accurately. Support processes, like process accelerators (catalysts and incubators), aid fine-tuning and are supplemented in Step 3 as required. In Step 2 the emphasis is on developing the core process.

Task 4: Finalizing the Business Plan

The aim of Task 4 is to draw up a business plan. The business plan of the market entry process *"company2newmarket"* differs perceptibly from traditional business plans in order to do justice to the specific requirements of a market entry project. Some of these differences are as follows: The business plan is based on the internationalization strategy of the company and its objectives. The plan contains all the specifications and assumptions on market entry strategy such as forms and timing as well as the existing resources, competences and competitive advantages. Thus the framework conditions for developing the business model are clearly defined. The second major aspect is the market. In this field, the most crucial market information that has been collected is stated, evaluated and analyzed and alternative courses of action are developed.

In the outline of the business model, the business plan concentrates mainly on the requisite adaptation to the target market. All the differences are identified in a GAP analysis and there are precise details of where the necessary competences and skills are to come from. This includes dealing with the lack of infrastructure (for example: no freight forwarders) or various distribution channels (for example: travelling traders as opposed to supermarkets). At the same time the reader ought to be able to understand how the market-specific challenges are to be met.

The financial plan within the business plan contains all the traditional instruments such as budgeted balance sheets, cash flow planning, investment and scenario analyses or balanced scorecards and is integrated in internal corporate planning and reporting tools. In addition there are also the specific tools for market entry projects. These comprise for example *process cost accounting,* which is crucial for assessing the performance of the individual steps, or *quota calculations* for analyzing the effectiveness of each activity in the core processes. These tools are crucial, for *you can only manage what you can measure.*

A tool that is a core element of added value is the *"Real-Option" Theory.* Due to its presence in a foreign market, therefore, a company has a real option to benefit from an above-average market growth. The best example of this is Volkswagen in China. Only by its presence for many years was it possible to become the market leader in China in line with economic growth. But a real option exists only if the company is present in the target market.

The price of the option consists mainly of market entry costs. If a company benefits from a favorable market development, the option is realized with a profit. If the foreign market – due for example to high political risks such as unrest – develops unfavorably or errors of one's own lead to a market exit, the option expires. The key factor in the "Real Option" Theory is that investments are regarded as an opportunity and not merely as costs.

The *project plan* within the business plan comprises the whole market entry process *"company2newmarket"* including all the costs, deadlines, activities, employees and objectives. Additional negative impacts from alterations to schedules and budgets are to be specified in scenario analyses. This also entails the likelihood of these occurring and measures to avoid negative deviations.

The initial business plan is based almost entirely on assumptions and experiences that are absolutely plausible and come from comparable projects of one's own or from other sources. However, all the figures are marked so that it is easy to recognize whether they are based on an assumption or on verified market knowledge. These result in the so-called *"knowledge to assumption ratio"*, which records the proportion of assumptions in the business plan and und how quickly the project management is in a position to replace these assumptions with verifiable knowledge.

The entire business plan is a living entity. It is not a static instrument but develops with every new piece of information. Above all, it constitutes a major information and communication medium particularly in such complex projects like international market entry. *Communication is motivation.* The business plan ought to be realistic according to the maxim: *Under-promise and over-deliver* – and not vice versa. Nevertheless, it must motivate to the extent that the management supports and wants to implement the project.

Step 2 "Market Preparation" is implemented individually for each foreign market. To this end each market is allocated a project of its own that has its own staff of project specialists.

Basically Step 2 "Market Preparation" is divided into four tasks whereby the right employees are selected first of all. These then establish the market positioning and draw up the process model and finally the business plan (including the financial plan). The focus is clearly on quality because errors cannot be rectified in the subsequent steps.

The tasks are carried out for as long as it takes to achieve the results that correspond to the internal requirements of the company. Thus the management is provided with a feasible business model as a comprehensive basis for decision-making. This business model is adopted in the subsequent step, Step 3 "Market Entry" and put into practice.

2.4. Step 3: Market Entry

Now things begin to get serious. For the first time there are visits to local customers or bars; and shops and branches welcome the first guests, who, it is to be hoped, will immediately become satisfied customers. In this Step 3 "Market Entry", too, licenses and authorizations are applied for, the infrastructure is built up and further local employees are hired and trained. All this takes place gradually as success on the market grows (Task 1).

The prototype of a business model resembles that of an engine. It is drawn up on the basis of the results in Task 2 and then tested. That means that measuring instruments are applied everywhere. It is like putting gas into an engine and then checking what horsepower it produces. In our business model, interested persons are contacted in the hope that at the end of the sales process the largest number of satisfied customers with the largest possible sales per head will have been acquired without having to invest too many resources.

Should the result not come up to expectations, further optimizations are undertaken until the target specifications are reached (Tasks 2 and 3). For this purpose, comprehensive control and measuring instruments are employed from the very beginning. One example of this is the Balanced Scorecard-Model that is expanded and adapted significantly to meet the requirements of international market entry.

The functioning prototype is the pattern for multiplication – i.e. only when this is functioning fully and extensively can multiplication take place. The criterion is profitable marketing of the products, i.e. profitability of the core processes. Again, it is also possible to compare it with an engine. It is only when it is running reliably and smoothly that it can be mass produced.

Task 1: Piloting of the Business Model

In most companies some time lapses between the completion of Step 2 and budget approval and the start of Step 3. Depending on the time lapse it is advisable to make a quick check whether the results of Step 2 are up to date before actually beginning Task 1, "Piloting of the Business Model".

According to the SPOT method the piloting of the business model involves testing the core processes without being able to fall back on the organization and technology that have been developed. This is a conscious decision. A high level of flexibility is crucial in the piloting stage because in all likelihood tests will be carried out on several prototypes. It is similar to tests on the test stand and is thus carried out mainly with provisional solutions. However, this does not affect the quality of the sales records, customer support and other elements crucial for success. This method needs to be highly professional because otherwise the results obtained will be useless.

There should be no compromises as far as control and measuring software are concerned. The data is collected in a controlling cockpit and measures all the activities of the core processes, their results and the duration of the tests. For example, a sales representative in Istanbul or Mumbai can only keep three of the five appointments planned per day due to the traffic situation but achieves the same results per appointment. Therefore alternative solutions such as telephone or internet sales need to be integrated and tested in the prototype. If that is not feasible, external, local wholesalers can be integrated into the project. Experienced project staff is crucial for this project phase. They have already found solutions in comparable situations and know how to make use of the comprehensive knowledge available in the company at any time.

The basis of all the evaluations in the controlling cockpit is an exact measurement of all the activities over different periods of time (see Table 8). That way information is gained not only about the duration of the sales process but also about the results of the modifications carried out.

Activity	Last week	Last month	Last quarter
Number of one's own contacts with interested persons			
Number of contacts by other means			
Number of initial appointments with interested persons			
Number of initial presentations carried out			
Number of second appointments kept (consultations)			
Number of offers			
Number of orders			
Number of cancellations /returns			
Number of consignments			

Table 8: Field worker's questionnaire

The evaluation chart (see Table 9) can be used for every employee and for the entire piloting. The evaluations provide deviations from the target figures that in turn are the basis for necessary improvement measures. The same system is used for core processes in administration.

The data from the controlling cockpit are fed directly into the business plan. On the basis of the products sold it is possible to calculate the first results and make further plans. At the same time a further reliable instru-

Activity according to various time frames	Achieved Result	Planned Result	Deviation	Benchmark Company	Best Practice Company
Number of one's own contacts with interested persons					
Number of contacts by other means					
Number of initial appointments with interested persons					
Number of initial presentations carried out					
Number of second appointments carried out					
Number of offers					
Number of orders					
Number of cancellations/ returns					
Number of consignments					

Table 9: Field worker's evaluation chart

ment is the phase model according to key profitability figures. Thus Step 3 aims at the profitability of the core processes and Step 4 aims at the operative profitability of the local company. The third key profitability figure is the profitability of the project which cannot usually be achieved within the market entry process "*company2newmarket*" due to the investments that have accrued.

Existing customers from other markets are particularly suitable for the piloting phase. They are prepared to act as samples or laboratory customers in return for a rebate, for having a say in the design of the product and naturally for additional product guarantees. This collaboration could even lead to a partnership developing. This model is especially appropriate for an industry with a relatively small number of end customers (for example: constructors of power stations, subcontractors to the automotive industry).

Like many other companies, Starbucks also works with the prototypes that can be seen in Tasks 1 and 2. After the business model stands, a small number of restaurants are opened in the new foreign market – independent of the market entry form. Internationally experienced restaurant managers train local employees, adapt the business model to local conditions, assign core competences and run the restaurants until these correspond to the global standards of the company. Parallel to this, local employees who have received initial training receive further training at headquarters where, apart from work-related issues, the main focus is on the corporate culture and "team spirit". Multiplication or the opening of further restaurants only takes place when all the prototypes have reached the targets set.

In the case of industrial companies with a B2B business model, internationalization starts at home. The objective is to win existing customers and gain contact to new customers (or even sample customers) in the new foreign market, customers who can then be used as references for winning local customers. In piloting the business model the global manager is grateful for every customer especially if there are already close contacts and mutual trust.

Task 2: Roll-out of the Business Model

In Task 2 the prototype that has been tested is launched onto the market. The processes of the prototypes that have been tested are adopted according to the SPOT concept, the organization is built round them and the (technological) infrastructure is supplemented. This task leads to a perceptible increase in fixed costs and in investments, too, without the corresponding revenue. Consequently, there is a significant increase in the risk.

The roll-out process can be compared to an aircraft taking off. Every source of energy is focused on the start to ensure that the aircraft can take off. The new local company has the same objective from an economic point of view. This requires high motivation and complete commitment from all local and international employees. Moreover, the project management (with the global manager) ought to concentrate on the most attractive products and on the greatest competitive advantages (for the market in question) with the aim of generating favorable contribution margins as soon as possible.

As with the aircraft, there can be turbulences during the steep ascent but no pilot will ever think of revising his objective unless there are technical difficulties. This should also apply to the global manager. First of all he should stay the course or if necessary he should switch on the afterburner by introducing marketing activities for example. As a result – after adapting the core process, for example a sales conversation with a customer – additional resources will be spent in order to achieve the planned objective.

Global managers and their local managing directors are regularly confronted with new challenges that need tackling. These can also be referred to as crises for even tiny errors can threaten the existence of the company or at least add perceptibly to the duration of this task. It is crucial to have a disciplined approach to implementing a permanent, gradual learning process. However, it is important not to lose sight of the overall picture on the one hand and not to forget the painstaking solution to many small problems on the other hand. Frequently the latter are underestimated. They can easily escalate and there is always someone in a company who thoroughly enjoys exploiting such omissions.

Here are some recommendations after some painful experiences:

- Global managers are not military conquerors wanting to hoist their flags everywhere as quickly as possible. First of all, they ought to concentrate on one region in the target market or on a selected number of flagship stores.
- Global managers ought to avoid secondary "battle fields", that means targeting a reduction in complexity.
- Global managers ought to focus on achieving and communicating swift successes. Information is motivation. Headquarters and all the employees are grateful for and take on board favorable information and continue to work together with greater motivation.
- Global managers ought to avoid well-known problems such as cancellations, bad debt losses or a dispute with customs authorities; they ought to solve and communicate other problems immediately. An escalation harms their careers and the projects.

- Global managers ought to keep the process model simple and understandable for as long as possible. This is helpful in multiplication and in implementing any adaptation that may prove necessary.
- Just as the light attracts moths, a new company attracts all kinds of people and wheeler-dealers expecting good business. From the beginning it is crucial, especially in a new market, not to trust the wrong people (Note: Usually these are the ones who claim to have the best contacts).
- In the operative stress of the roll-out phase very important learning processes take place which should, on no account, be passed on. It is the global manager's task to carry out training regularly and to ensure the exchange of information.

It is difficult to impart the challenges of a roll-out to managers from the homeland. Unlike the home market, the brand and the company are usually entirely unknown in the target market. However, it is particularly in the roll-out phase that the new local company relies on every recommendation and every customer enquiry. Apart from the traditional advertising media (a must for every company) such as a website presence, a company presentation and a highly informative product catalogue with fact sheets on the individual products in the language of the country in question, the following tools are very helpful because they can produce results relatively quickly:

- Winning over local opinion leaders as a "way-in", as consultants and a source of recommendations;
- Using testimonials by local celebrities as advertising media;
- Certifications from recognized sources such as local research institutes or universities;
- Recommendations from existing contacts and customers (worldwide).

Task 3: Modifications to Roll-Outs

After the roll-out of the core processes it is the function of Task 3 to examine whether the benchmarks demanded have been achieved and to introduce appropriate measures in the case of deviations. These functions are also part of Task 2. However, practice has shown that it is useful to carry out modifications to the roll-out separately. It is usually adaptations to the business model in particular that impact the company strategy and the business plan. On the one hand these adaptations cannot be decided by the project management and on the other hand they are usually not essential. A separate task affords the "view from the outside" and can develop specific alternative courses of action.

The existing control instruments enable the global manager to see the exact cause of the problems: Are there not enough potential customers in the shop? Are there too many customers that are not buying enough? Are they buying different products to what was expected? Is the cost of acquiring new customers too high? Are the rates of repeated sales too low? This data enables the global manager to decide whether there is a fundamental error in the business model, whether the model simply needs more volume until for example economies of scale take effect or whether motivation needs boosting.

If there is a fundamental error the global manager has to be consistent and return to Step 2 in order to make modifications to the business and process model. Under no circumstances should there be any muddling along out of fear of a confrontation with reality or repairs to the symptoms according to the motto: "Hope is the last to die". Simple and swift compromises are not a solution. This is not an easy decision to make. From experience, the local project manager and future head of the overseas branch office is more likely to propagate stronger adaptation to the foreign market as a solution whereas head office will prefer to rely on greater use of their own competitive advantages.

The last-mentioned conflict is solved by setting up several branch offices in the target market in parallel (precondition: sufficient market potential). If all the branches are faced with the same challenges, the business model will need optimizing urgently. If at least one branch develops better than expected, the global manager has significant proof of success and has gained a model for the others.

If it is more likely that the necessary sales volume is missing or the expected growth is not high enough, the overseas branch can be raised with an afterburner to a higher level in the long term. An afterburner operates as with aircraft whereby extra energy – for example in the form of investments in marketing activities – is added and this acts like a catalyst (process accelerator). An afterburner is also an option for activity if there is no overseas branch to assume the role of a model and thus counteract any potential demotivation with this measure. However, a precondition for this is that the business model functions otherwise money for the afterburner is wasted.

The task of Step 3 is market entry or the practical implementation of the business model in the foreign market whereby Step 3 builds solely on the results of Step 2. It is only if this step is successful that an expansion can be started in the target market. On the basis of the necessary modifications the company receives, for the first time, direct feedback on the quality of the preparations in the preceding Steps 1 and 2.

Step 3 consists of three tasks and starts with piloting. This is followed by roll-out and modifications to the roll-out including a potential "afterburner". Completing Step 3 means that the first step to market entry has been successful. The aircraft has gained altitude, is flying more smoothly and is kept aloft by increasing thermal currents.

Setting up the local network can now begin, too. Contacts are only harmful to those who do not have any, and that means you as global manager. You know hardly anyone, do not receive any information, are not in a position to assess this and do not really know what is to be done. That can be very dangerous for a company. The company management needs to know how to respond to the market and how to deal with the various stakeholders.

Step 3 again illustrates strikingly how crucial it is to implement a market entry process like "company2newmarket". It supports the global manager in making better decisions, in using fewer resources and in achieving good results more quickly. Its flexibility as an iterative learning process also helps to meet new challenges in a very professional way.

2.5. Step 4: Market Development and Growth

Usually this final but no less important step is simply ignored. This is hard to understand because it is precisely the skill to wind up unprofitable overseas branch offices at a reasonable price and to implement market growth strategies successfully that is often known as the high art of international management.

Global managers are extremely happy when they have reached the break-even point in a foreign market. Therefore, the organizational integration into the group management structure is executed before the skill to "stand alone" and the planned size of the company have been achieved. This is absolutely irresponsible and negligent because the small company simply does not have the management structures and the economic resources to establish a sustainably stable market position in its foreign market through internal and external growth.

A further topic that everyone shirks is market exit. This is often seen as a failure which is frequently punished in many cultures with a stigma that permeates an entire career. Yet it is precisely the opposite that is the case. Framework conditions in markets can change. We can see in North Africa, Southern Europe or Argentina in particular that it is not a matter of failure but quite simply the securing of assets, the reduction of risks and the avoidance of losses and therefore there is a great deal of money at stake.

A very special challenge and a major task is localizing management and decentralizing competences to the overseas company. There is a similarity to the relationship between a mother and child. A young person is only capable of surviving if it leads its own life. Applied to a subsidiary the local management has to gradually adapt the business model with regard to its products and services to the foreign market and its culture as growth increases; that means that the local company becomes a "good corporate citizen". When there are problems (and something can always be found in young companies) the mother is not willing to grant her child the necessary freedom and the manager of head office is unwilling to hand over competences. A great deal of political and diplomatic skill, quite a bit of persuasion and a competent decision-making body are required.

Task 1: Promoting Internal Growth

The objective of Step 3 is the profitability of the core process. In Step 3 a manufacturer of vacuum cleaners, for example, is concerned with the profitable sale of the vacuum cleaners in the target market. In Step 4 the profitability of the entire business model is to the fore. First of all the global manager in conjunction with his country manager will multiply the core process by hiring further sales persons, supplementing the new products (for example with vacuum cleaner bags and industrial vacuum cleaners), open further distribution channels (for example web shops and retail markets) and open branches in further towns and regions. This course of action is also referred to as internal growth (Task 1). In this way, a company continues to invest in its subsidiary in order to achieve the market position it desires with respect to sales and profitability. The internal growth targets are part of the "handover" criteria that on the one hand define the ability of the subsidiary to stand alone and on the other hand define the completion of the project.

All further core, support and management processes are introduced in this first task. In practice this means that apart from the core products tested in Step 3 all the products and services planned for the foreign market are offered, too. Naturally this also includes all the marketing activities necessary for market entry and services such as a guarantee and repair service.

Parallel to this the market entry region (for example Shanghai, Mumbai, São Paulo or Istanbul) is developed before a country-wide expansion takes place. This means that new shops are opened regionally and new sales persons hired. According to the motto "Anyone who doesn't succeed in Shanghai won't succeed in other parts of China either", experience is gained, to start with, in the market that is worked first and attempts are made to achieve the operative break-even point. It is only af-

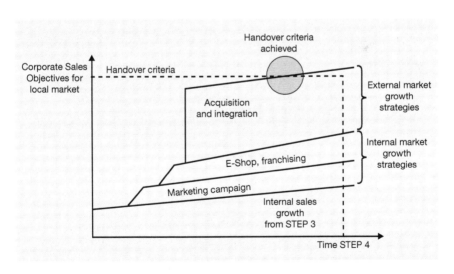

Fig. 29: Interaction of internal and external market growth forms

ter that that the company goes to other cities and other regions of the country.

Internal and external market growth forms are used to achieve growth (see Fig. 29). They are comparable to market entry forms. However, the conditions are different under which they are used. In this phase of the project the company knows the foreign market better which therefore permits the choice of riskier market growth forms.

Tools for promoting internal growth are the so-called "build" market growth forms. These are very similar to the market entry forms and are described in detail there. A combination of these is especially interesting for internal growth. Thus every extra customer and every extra day in the new foreign market afford the company valuable additional information whereby the "knowledge-to-assumption" ratio rises and the risks of more capital intensive market growth forms such as subsidiaries decline.

The following examples show the advantages of this concept:

- A company that only exports to one foreign market at first plans to establish a sales branch as success increases and experience grows. There the number of sales persons is increased gradually and as the customer portfolio grows, guarantees and a repair service and even assembly are offered.
- A company first of all licenses its products or technology to a local company. As success and market attractiveness grow, the licensor might decide to acquire the licensee. A similar approach is also advisable with joint ventures. Purchasing the company shares of the local joint venture partner has advantages for both parties. The local entrepreneur gets a reasonable price for the risk and work he had in setting up the branch. The company has a perceptibly lower market entry risk.
- A further internal market growth form is the parallel market entry into several regions such as St. Petersburg and Moscow in Russia or New York, Los Angeles and other cities in the USA.

Every company ought to concentrate on the market growth forms that are best suited to its business model and in which it has expertise. In practice, it has transpired that this usually amounts to two or three at most. In addition to internal growth forms a company also has external ones at its disposal. These are expected to generate greater sales volume in order to benefit from economies of scale and other synergies. Companies with sustainable competitive advantages in production technology for example can thus make faster use of their advantage.

Task 2: Promoting External Growth

External growth is regarded critically by many global managers. Many see it as an admission that their own objectives cannot be achieved through internal growth alone. Others point to the high risks that an acquisition and the subsequent integration entail. Nevertheless, external growth options need to be subject to continual screening, as the example of Nestlé in China shows. It was only after the purposeful acquisition of Chinese companies that have a better understanding of local customer requirements that the world's largest food manufacturer succeeded in establishing an adequate market position in the largest market in the world.

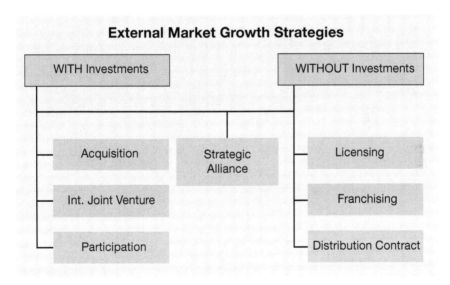

External Market Growth Strategies

Fig. 30: External market growth forms

An external growth strategy does not simply mean acquisitions. Growth forms such as licensing, franchising or an alliance are particularly appropriate for companies that (at the moment) do not wish to make large additional investments in the foreign market in question. Thus a comprehensive market entry can take place via a franchise concept or a distribution agreement (an internationally strategic alliance) with local wholesalers. In contrast, establishing one's own distribution organization would take considerably longer and would be perceptibly more expensive.

A four-step process (see Fig. 31) has proved successful in implementing external growth alternatives. In the first step, the global manager has to check whether the requisite conditions exist: Is the new local overseas branch in a position to implement external growth alternatives in an operational and responsible way? Are the appropriate HR and economic resources – with the support of head office, too – in place? It is precisely in this business phase that there is a danger of dispersal and overburdening which can endanger the young company. Moreover, there are often diverging interests between the global manager and the new local management.

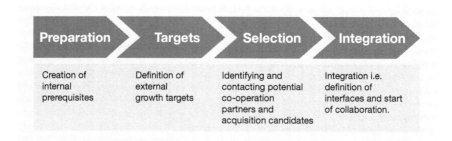

Fig. 31: Process for implementing external market growth strategies

The objectives for using external growth alternatives are usually market-driven. Customer portfolios, distribution channels and future sales are acquired by means of co-operations and takeovers. Furthermore, there are also resource-driven objectives such as the acquisition of additional competences or the establishing of extra cost advantages especially in new international markets. That way prevailing barriers to market entry can be overcome. An acquisition is often opportunity-driven, too; that means that a favorable opportunity to purchase simply presents itself. Doubtlessly such opportunities ought to be examined seriously and very carefully. That way, purely opportunity-driven international-ization strategies always fail in the long run.

The first difficult challenge is selecting the right co-operation partners. It is advisable for global managers to check reputations and integrity in addition to purely economic data – just the way it is done in purchasing and distribution. Collaboration with local wholesalers outside the core markets is particularly appropriate for small local companies in major foreign markets.

By far the greatest challenge is integration – i.e. daily collaboration. Whereas in the case of an acquisition the management and the M & A department can celebrate the "wedding" and thus the completion of the project, the global and country managers have to live together "in matrimony". It is here that many come to grief as can be seen in the large number of depreciations.

Task 3: Localizing Management and Integrating into the Management Structure

Localizing management means handing over responsibility to local managers whereby the project staff belonging to the company (usually expatriates or transpatriates) are gradually relieved of their functions as soon as they have taught a local successor the ropes and have passed on the requisite skills and information. This also applies to the global manager who together with the country manager usually forms the project management. This task is crucial because the local management now has an opportunity to integrate the subsidiary into the local economy and society more effectively and handing over responsibility can trigger a surge in motivation among the local employees and executives.

This task is often referred to as "handover management". At the end, the global manager uses a checklist to discover whether the new local company has met all the requirements of this "stand-alone" ability. These are for example the sustainability of the business model, the existence of all the authorizations and the requisite indicators (sales, customers, locations), the complete staffing of executive committees, stable growth of sales and adequate profitability, the necessary capital and the implementation of the necessary control and management processes (quality management, controlling, risk control). Documentation of the "handover protocol" is crucial for the completion of the project and the commencement of activities by the new executive committees.

As soon as the local management has assumed its function, integration into the corporate management structure takes place. This can also be seen as the handover by the project management to the operational contact persons in the group. Thus the local book-keeper is networked with the central financial department, the local purchasing manager with the central export department or the respective IT and marketing departments with one another.

At the same time, the local board of non-executive directors assumes its responsibilities. This includes for example defining the strategy and implementing the management-, communication-, information- and reporting processes The local board of non-executive directors mainly consists of managers within the group, whereby integrating an external local opinion leader is to be strongly recommended.

It is in this phase that the local management learns its ambivalent bridging function between an international company and the local market. It needs to find a symbiosis between the standards within the group that have to be accepted without further ado and the requirements of the local market. Those executives who have grown up in both cultures generally do well in this respect.

Task 4: Completion of the Project

The final task is the completion of the project. Its core task is preparing the documentation of the project. This includes among other things all the protocols such as the "handover" protocol and preparing a final report on the project.

The final report on the project summarizes the results of the project:

- The attainment of the project objectives whereby all the time delays, economic and HR deviations and differences in content including modifications during the course of the project are stated and substantiated;

- The handover protocol that contains among other things the checklist as to the ability of the new local company to "stand alone", the localizing of the management and integration into the entire company;
- The experiences and perceptions (learning transfer into the organization) which ought to be documented and made available to similar projects and employees who, within the organization, have contact to the new local company. This also applies to the market monitor and the cultural profile;
- The completion and final control of all the tasks; record of points still open, follow-up work and risks;
- The acceptance by the steering committee and the principal.

The completion of the project also entails a debriefing for all the employees engaged on the project. This usually takes place in the form of an event that includes a small celebration.

At this point at the latest, all internal project staff ought to have been entrusted with new responsibilities. It is certainly easiest for those members of the staff working on the project temporarily and still attached to their organization. A great challenge is the placing of experienced expatriates, who frequently suffer from a repatriation shock upon their return to the home country. It is hardly possible to integrate them into traditional organizations, to find a further transfer that might be appropriate or to allow them to stay in the last target country. As a result, the majority of qualified executives leave the company in frustration within two years of their transfer abroad.

The potential laid down in the first three steps is realized in Step 4 "Market Development and Growth". A company is developed that in the event of an exit will have a value.

An attractive and sustainable market position can be established successfully with internal and external growth. This also includes launching all the processes and products onto and adapting them to the local market.

Furthermore, a management structure is set up that can combine the two extremes of adapting to the local market and integrating into a global organization. It consists primarily of local executives who are used to working in international companies.

The project management's last task is integration into the corporate management structure and thus constitutes the completion of the market entry process *"company2newmarket"*. The global manager will continue to fall back on tools such as the IMM *International Market Monitor*, the implementation of market growth forms and the market exit process as required.

2.6. Carrying out Market Exits

Market entries also entail market exits. Global managers need to master market exits, too. This unpopular and usually extremely thankless task is part and parcel of the global manager's tools of the trade. Market exits that are implemented in a professional manner save a great deal of money and secure reputations. A market exit has to be expected after each step of the market entry process *"company2newmarket"* has been completed if the objectives planned are not achieved or there is a change in the market conditions.

A market exit is not an admission of errors. In point of fact, market exits are part of the global manager's daily business. In the event of political or economic crises in Argentina for example or in the MENA and GIPS countries, global managers have to act swiftly and bring the employees and assets to safety. To that end it is essential that they are well prepared for the emergency and that on entering the market they know how to get out again.

The basis of any market exit is a clearly defined process with the requisite steps, tasks and tools. An example of this is presented in this section.

Reasons for Market Exits

Although there are not many reliable figures on the long-term relationship between market entries and market exits, available studies show that ca. 50 percent of all market entry projects are discontinued sooner or later whereby no distinction is made as to whether the entire project was economically successful or whether there were internal or external reasons for the market exit. Nevertheless it can be conjectured that the majority of the market entry projects were discontinued due to a lack of success or due to one of the following causes:

- *Deterioration of market attractiveness* reduces the enterprise value of the subsidary; sales and profits drop whereas claims rise simultaneously. This leads to (full) depreciation for the enterprise value in the consolidated balance sheet. Market attractiveness can drop for the following reasons:
- Increased political risk (current examples: political revolutions and changes in MENA = Middle East / North Africa)
- Deterioration of economic framework conditions (current example: the debt crisis in Europe with immense impact on the competitiveness of the GIPS countries (Greece, Italy, Portugal, Spain)
- Increasing legal uncertainty due to (de-facto) expropriation, regulation, increases in taxes and duties, and political pressure on entrepreneurs (current example: Argentina and France, too)
- *Strategic decisions* often lead to the sale or closure of subsidiaries (for example by relocating resources from stagnating sales markets to global growth markets). In many cases the local management takes over the company with a management buy-out. That way a certain measure of continuity is ensured for customers and employees.
- *Miscalculations and management errors* in market entry projects are a further huge source of market exits, as the following examples show:
- Discontinuation of the market entry project, for instance as a result of underestimating the cultural differences, a lack of infrastructure or wrong HR policy (for example: employment of key expatriates abroad is discontinued because the families cannot or do not wish to integrate)
- Irreconcilable conflicts with IJV/ISA partners for example in matters of technology; the IJV partner desires a transfer of technology whereas the company only wishes to continue to market its "old" technologies via the IJV
- The integration of an acquisition does not reach the targets wished for on account of cultural differences and the retirement of the key managers (including the ex-proprietor). Sales slump. The company operates at a loss.

The IMM International Market Monitor as an Early Warning System

Market exits cost a company a great deal of money. In addition there are opportunity costs. If only one market exit can be avoided or delayed by the early warning system, the investment has paid off.

The *IMM International Market Monitor* regularly measures the market attractiveness of a country according to clearly defined criteria. These are suitable as early indicators. Further criteria can be added as required.

The *IMM International Market Monitor* measures external risks and in particular the political and economic changes that impact companies. Internal risks ought to be recorded via the prevailing risk-management systems.

The aim of the *IMM International Market Monitor* is the early recognition of changes and crises so that a company can adapt to their consequences. Companies use this information to allocate their resources efficiently across foreign markets. In Fig. 32 the key performance indicators slump and although they recover later, they remain below the target range. The simplest solution is to adapt the targets to the new reality. However, this usually costs perceptibly more money and does not improve the situation. After a report by the *IMM International Market Monitor*, the measures are adapted in order to achieve the targets.

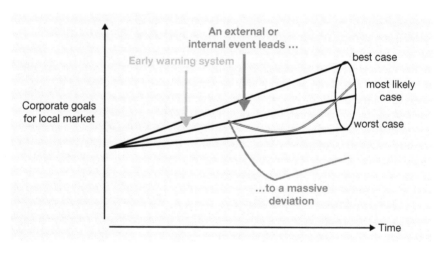

Fig. 32: Benefits of early warning systems when entering foreign markets

If the return to the target range fails and it seems unlikely that the project will achieve the expected targets in the long term, the global manager ought to contemplate a market exit.

In addition to a sophisticated early warning system there is also a whole series of simple, practical tips which every global manager should bear in mind as the following examples show:

- Always keep liquid assets in head office ("cash-pooling");
- Avoid bad debts entirely by ensuring that every project and every customer is always "cash positive" (in many countries legal action is arduous and expensive);
- Replace warehousing in foreign markets with regional logistics hubs in countries with low political risk;
- Bundle IP rights (intellectual property rights) in a specialized company in locations with low political risk and attractive taxation;
- Separate central R & D from local application development, and repairs and assembly especially in the case of partnerships with other companies (for example: joint venture);
- Pursue an uncompromising anti-corruption policy;
- Obviously comply with all the laws; but also develop a corporate culture with its own values and guidelines for operations in order to be particularly well prepared in dubious situations.

Structure of a Market Exit Process

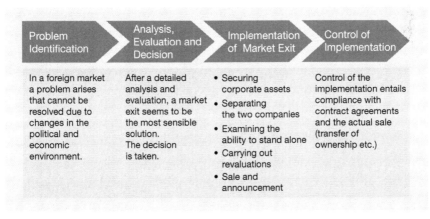

Fig. 33: Market exit process in four steps

As soon as the global manager has identified a huge problem via his early warning system, a structured market exit process begins. This can consist of four steps: identification of the problem; analysis, evaluation and decision; implementation of the market exit and control of the result/implementation (see Fig. 33).

Preparing for Market Exit

In the second phase the global manager establishes alternative courses of action. Apart from continuing with the management of and the restructuring of the overseas company, the various market exit scenario are to the fore. If the market exit is planned within the first three steps of the market entry process *"company2newmarket"*, liquidation or the resale of the company shell with the accumulated deficit carried forward is advisable. This task is usually delegated to a specialized liquidator in collaboration with the local authorities.

As of Step 4 of the market entry process *"company2newmarket"*, the overseas company has customers, sales, employees and structures that represent a certain value. Thus the sale of the overseas company becomes a realistic alternative. At this stage, only the management itself and with reservations customers, competitors and suppliers are worth considering as potential purchasers.

The acquisition of the overseas company by the management is referred to as an MBO (management buy-out); as soon as it has been financed with a credit, it is also referred to as an LBO (leveraged buy-out). An MBO is an attractive alternative for both parties. The management preserves its position, the employees keep their jobs and the enterprise still has a distribution partner in this foreign market. At the same time it reduces its risks and might even receive a little money which can then be invested in more attractive foreign markets.

Implementing the Market Exit

The first step is to *take stock*. The global manager has an interim balance sheet prepared and records all the assets of the company such as real estate, bank balances, the value of stocks or intellectual property (for example: trademark rights, patents). Due to the wide-spread centralization of cash and property management, warehousing and the right to intellectual property there are usually no great assets to be found.

In the second step, the overseas company is separated from the parent company. In the case of this *separation* all legal constructs have to be disentangled (for example: profit and loss transfer agreements, guarantees, and letters of comfort). Furthermore, decisions have to be taken as to which assets and employees will remain in the company.

These decisions have a considerable impact on the third step: examining *the "stand alone" ability*. It must be ascertained whether the company is capable of acting on the market autonomously and successfully. This presupposes that all the necessary licenses, rights and authorizations are in place; supply contracts in line with the market have been concluded with the (former) parent company; leases have been made over to the overseas company and there are sufficient financial resources.

In many cases further *upgrading measures* have to be carried out. These are economic concessions by the parent company to make the transition easier for the new owners. Examples of these are the licensing of rights, a waiver of claims, loss assumption for the next business year, an extension of the credit periods, the financing of marketing activities or payment of the purchasing price in installments. In return the parent company ought to have a clause included in the agreement whereby a (re)purchase option with a fixed formula for calculating the purchase price is possible in subsequent years.

When both contracting parties have reached an agreement, the *contract is signed* and all stakeholders are informed.

Controlling the implementation of the market exit

A major point is controlling the implementation of the market exit. In conclusion, the global manager needs to make sure that the parent company is discharged from all obligations and that the property is transferred correctly to the company.

The professional management of market exits saves a great deal of money, protects the corporate reputation and helps to increase the profitability and prestige of the overseas company. For that reason it is the global manager's responsibility to prepare for the market exit and to set up the requisite competences and tools.

By definition market exits are neither good nor bad. Market exit with the sale of one's own subsidiary can be very profitable but if it is the result of management errors or political changes it can also mean considerable losses.

The framework conditions in a foreign market usually change slowly so that a company has time to make thorough preparations for market exit and to implement these. Nevertheless, it should also be prepared for sudden changes such as wars and revolutions. Consequently, country risks ought to be subject to constant evaluation. This particularly applies to the access to resources (for example: rare earths and other raw materials) or production (for example: local-content regulations, data protection), the safety of logistics routes (for example: piracy), the choice of providers (for example: Foxconn/Apple) and the observation of the principles of the UN Global Compact and the quality assurance thereof.

The decision in favor of a market exit is usually only taken when the worst is over. Early warning systems such as the *IMM International Market Monitor* help with taking decisions in good time and introducing appropriate measures with plans already prepared for contingencies. In the case of market exit swift implementation and professional communication are advisable.

Summary

The objective of a process for international market entry is winning new customers in new international markets in a shorter time, with fewer resources and fewer risks. This objective is reached by an efficient and structured approach that on the one hand entails a transparent sequence of steps and tasks and on the other hand uses efficient tools. In this way the international market entry is professionalized and can be multiplied. This means that several new foreign markets can be opened up simultaneously and more efficiently.

With the steady use of a process for international market entry, the internationalization of a company gradually becomes a key core competence or a sustainable competitive advantage that determines its global market position. Today, only those companies that are in a position to sell innovative technologies and new products on major international markets faster and more successfully than their competitors can prevail in global competition.

An important, perhaps even the most important reason for using a process for international market entry is to avoid expensive failures. For this reason, the profitability of an international organization rises significantly; the cost of international market entry decreases perceptibly. At the same time, the good reputation of the company remains intact thanks to the fact that there are fewer failures. The professional implementation of market exits is also a key factor here.

Companies implementing a market entry process like "*company2newmarket*" consistently and sustainably have developed purposefully to "hidden champions" or to global market leaders in their relevant markets. Global managers play a major role. They have to develop the international market entry process skillfully into a flexible and adaptive instrument and at the same time counteract all the formalization tendencies of bureaucratic organizations.

Lessons to be learned

1. *Be consistent in implementing the market entry process "company2newmarket"*. It supplies you with an overall view; it is your cockpit abroad for, in cases of doubt, your knowledge and experiences count for nothing there.
2. *Be quick to learn*. Among other things, international market entry is about gaining and processing information. Always optimize your "knowledge-to-assumption ratio".
3. *Avoid typical risks*. In addition to traditional market entry risks new overseas companies are particularly subject to bad debt losses and loss of IP.
4. *People make the difference here. Win the right employees*. Selecting the right employees and management is half the battle and accounts for more than 50 percent of the success of your project.

5. *Ensure the high-quality of your data.* "Garbage-in, garbage-out!" This rule also applies abroad. It is difficult to obtain high-quality data; therefore, it is all the more important to take the greatest care.

6. *Become a specialist in market exits.* That way you prevent high costs and spectacular failures.

7. *Internationalization begins at home.* Win existing customers and contacts as new and test customers for the new foreign market and ensure you have the support of the parent company.

8. *Develop products with test customers.* Potential customers are usually very frank if they are offered a development partnership. Collaboration is often to be had for a rebate and if their own requirements are met.

9. *Pay attention to a high level of start-up culture and to motivation in the project team.* There is a saying that a glass is either half full or half empty. The perspective can change many things and it can topple very quickly in market entry projects.

10. *Communication is motivation.* Under-promise and over-deliver: If you promise too much, your project will quickly become suspect; never promise what you cannot keep.

11. *Reconcile "global strategy" with "local responsiveness".* It is not a matter of compromises but of a symbiotic and synergetic collaboration that uses the strengths of both extremes successfully.

12. *Develop a clear strategy and implement it consistently.* Pure opportunity-driven internationalization strategies need revising sooner or later. Actually, this always involves high costs and calls all overseas activities into question.

13. *Make use of the SPOT concept*: Always work according to the sequence: strategy, process, organization and technology.

14. *Beware of dubious profiteers especially in the beginning*: A large number of people will get in touch with you. Don't trust everyone right away.

15. *International management is always intercultural management, too.* The skill of dealing with other cultures makes crucial demands on the global manager and the local project manager.

16. *The myth of globalizing – the reality of regionalizing*: for years this applied particularly to small and medium sized businesses that expanded primarily in the European Union. The debt crisis is driving them out of Europe in a development from regional sales markets to global growth markets.

3. Intercultural Management – More Efficient Management of Global Organizations with Intercultural Intelligence

International management is always intercultural management, too. Today, dealing with employees and customers from diverse cultural groups does not just begin at national borders but usually starts in the workforce. Increasingly, these groups portray great diversity with regards to age, education, race, religion and with greater frequency to cultural and linguistic background.

Thus each employee and most certainly each executive ought to have an awareness of cultural differences and knowledge thereof. With this in mind, I have created cultural profiles, which I have branded "intercultural intelligence", for the major cultures and countries (see Section 3.4.). These cultural profiles are tools for global managers and all employees who come into contact with other cultures. They contain basic information on the country and the culture of a conversation partner and can be called up anytime and anywhere.

Cultural profiles are based on existing and well-tried cultural models. The best known theories which were propounded some decades ago are presented in Section 3.2. Their findings have been expanded and checked constantly and today they are well-known all over the world. Cultural profiles are created on the basis of the cultural differences derived from these theories (see Section 3.3) and offer recommendations that are easy to understand and implement. Understanding these requires cultural sensitivity and for this reason communication skill in an intercultural environment. Its ultimate aim is achieving one's own objectives.

The highlight of this chapter is Section 3.5 which deals with corporate culture caught between individual national cultures. A global corporation always finds itself between the culture of its country of origin, the various cultures of its employees and those of the foreign markets being developed. In this environment it has to develop its own culture by integrating the diverse cultures symbiotically and synergistically in a melting pot so to speak. First of all, however, I would like to address some intercultural misunderstandings.

3.1. Some Facts about Culture

Ever since politics began to address the subject of culture, there have been continual efforts in the name of "political correctness" to deny the existence of cultural differences or at least to play down their significance. However, such efforts are out of touch with reality and get us nowhere. It is by no means a question of prejudices, stereotype or discrimination but exclusively tools and methods to understand and respect cultural diversity and to improve intercultural communication.

Cultural Types

Global managers are always faced with intercultural challenges. In addition to their own culture they have to bear in mind the diverse national cultures of their project staff, the culture of the foreign market, of their own corporation, the industry and frequently the various professional groups, too. There are also cultural differences within individual professional groups: the typical sales person is different from the typical bookkeeper, engineer, programmer or lawyer. In technical occupations in particular, which have their own language and globally recognized rules, intercultural communication functions surprisingly well. This chapter deals exclusively with the differences between the cultures of different countries – i.e. culture as the expression of the life of a nation in its entirety. In the subsequent sections this will be referred to as national culture.

Cultures are relative

A culture portrays the learned behavior of a foreign market according to unwritten laws. There are sub-cultures in every group or in every country. Thus you find that in Spain Catalans and the Basques are different from Madrilenians, in Germany Bavarians are different from Prussians, in Italy South-Tyrolese are different from Sicilians and in Switzerland French-speaking Swiss are different from German-speaking Swiss. Nevertheless, subcultures are still part of a common culture. They have for example a common language, a common history and the same institutions.

Extreme characteristics as in the extroverted bookkeeper and the introverted sales person can be found in every culture. Therefore, every individual in a culture has his own personality. Cultures are always relative. As a result they always describe a group of people but not an individual. Cultures exist only in relation to each other. A national culture exists only by comparison with another national culture.

Cultures are Different

Other cultures are different – neither better nor worse, but simply different. Comparing cultural differences and dealing with different cultures does not mean evaluating but only understanding the differences. The task that the manager of an intercultural project team has is ensuring good collaboration in intercultural organizations whereby cultural differences frequently clash. A good manager succeeds in combining the strengths of the individual cultures symbiotically and synergistically and does not submit to unsatisfactory compromises.

The myth of a "global" culture

Time and again, as globalization has increased, there have been forecasts that this will lead to a global culture. The success story of global corporations like McDonald's, Coca-Cola, Apple or Facebook and Hollywood film companies that represent part of the American lifestyle and spread it all over the world, is supposed to underpin this thesis. However, using a product has very little to do with the culture of a country or a region and is unlikely to change these.

The same applies to most expatriates. Today the vast majority of people still spend all their lives in their home land. Exceptions are usually a stay abroad while studying or during the first years in one's profession. But as soon as a move up the career ladder or family planning is in the offing, then it is usually a case of returning to the home land. Abroad the expats live, for the most part, with their families in communities, meet in their own clubs and send their children to international schools. Under such circumstances, the cultural exchange with the host country remains limited.

Adapting to cultures

What can be expected from employees who are sent to another country? Obviously they are not expected to change their culture, their values or their attitudes but they ought to adapt their behavior so that they solve professional tasks successfully. This expectation assumes that people can learn behavior, such as body language, lifestyle, eating and drinking habits or dress codes. Moreover, global managers can expect these employees to learn the language of the country in question. That is the key to the culture of the host country.

As soon as they are back in their home country, they will revert to their former behavior. Thus Swiss employees sent to China will adapt to the culture there and upon their return to Switzerland will revert to their original behavior. It is just the same for an Egyptian who has completed a course of technical studies in the USA. After his return he will make use of his technical knowledge within the framework of his own culture.

One's own culture

As far as global managers are concerned, the world is their home. However, they ought not to forget their roots and their own culture. Chinese global managers will always be Chinese. In Brazil they will not become Brazilian and in France they won't become French and that is not expected of them. But they do need to be able to adapt their behavior so that they are capable of working with Brazilians and French. At the same time, they remain Chinese. That is what their business partners also expect. That means that they are authentic and predictable for all their business partners.

Self-reference criteria

Every person understands what another person wishes to communicate against the background of his own culture. As a result, even simple statements can be understood in different ways. That can lead to misunderstandings. This is unavoidable and applies especially to non-verbal communication. According to Freud's "Iceberg"-Theory, only ten percent of a national culture can be recognized, for example, by it symbols and rituals. The remaining 90 percent – consisting of values and beliefs – disappears below the surface and is hardly perceptible. Intercultural management is about better understanding – i.e. using tools to improve the efficiency of the mutual communication and collaboration of all parties concerned.

Culture and leadership styles

In intercultural research on leadership styles a distinction is made between universalists and culturalists. The former are of the opinion that there is only one correct leadership style independent of all cultures; the latter emphasize the dependence on the culture in question. In practice the truth is somewhere in between. The more abstract, technical and higher in the hierarchy a function or tool is, the better it can be standardized globally. On the one hand this is due to the tasks of and on the other hand to the intercultural education of international executives. Good examples of this are to be found in functions such as finance, project management and reporting. Vice versa, the influence of the culture increases as soon as people are involved. Nevertheless, every employee – and every executive – is part of a culture to which individual behavior is geared.

Cultural differences do exist and it is important for global managers to be aware of this. Only then can they achieve their objectives by behaving in the appropriate manner in their professional environment and by using the strengths of the individual cultures. The integration of individual employees into a corporation is achieved by schooling the behavior that is desired and that at the same time shows respect for the culture of every single employee.

3.2. Dimensions of National Cultures

The behavior of people from different cultures is influenced by various factors. In his "Layer Model of Environmental Differentiation", Eberhard Dülfer depicts in full all the factors that influence the behavior of the individual and explains these from the history of globalization. Other cultural models go one step further. They aim at describing cultures on the basis of the results measured in different cultural dimensions. These results are used to demonstrate the differences between two cultures. Regrettably, all the cultural models use diverse cultural dimensions so that the results are difficult to compare and do not always complement each other.

So far there has been no success in developing a universal cultural model or uniting diverse cultural models with each other. Moreover, the models are relatively static. Naturally both these points restrict their validity. Despite these limitations the results could be confirmed and supported in many studies. Their significance lies in the fact that this is the first attempt at making diverse cultures comparable and awaking greater sensitivity and respect in people who have contacts to other cultures when they meet with different behavior.

Eberhard Dülfer's Layer Model

Dülfer shows in his "Layer Model of Environmental Differentiation" which influences impact on the behavior of a foreigner engaged in conversation with a global manager. The individual layers – "natural facts", "the level of technology", "moral concepts", "social relations", "legal and political standards" and "tasks environment" build upon one another and continually influence each other. The model is dynamic. Changes in individual layers (for example: the natural disaster of the tsunami in Japan) impact on all the other layers (for example: adaptation of the energy supply and legislation).

With his "Layer Model of Environmental Differentiation" Dülfer succeeds in compiling a complete record and description of all the factors that have an impact. In particular he proves how historical events long ago shape the current behavior of foreign customers and employees. His publications offer decidedly interesting reading to anyone keen to learn about the history of globalization.

Compared with Dülfer's model, the studies on cultural dimensions described below go one step further when they try to measure the differences between two cultures using different cultural dimensions.

Cultural dimensions according to Edward T. Hall

Edward T. Hall is a US anthropologist who is well-known for his research on intercultural communication. In the course of his work he attempted to define intercultural misunderstandings on the basis of the four dimensions of national culture which he had developed: proxemics, high versus low context, monochronic versus polychronic, and the ability of cultures to process information quickly. Unlike subsequent cultural models he developed and publicized his cultural dimensions step-by-step.

Cultural Dimension	Definition
Proxemics	This dimension portrays the independently various, large distance zones that people permit or rather which they try to protect against "intruders" in different ways. A distinction is made between intimate, personal, social and public distance zones.
High vs. low context	In cultures with a low context, it is usual to be absolutely frank and call a spade a spade. There is the feeling of being obliged to give precise information to the person vis-à-vis. In cultures with high context, knowledge of many details is assumed by implication and mentioning them can be experienced as negative.
Mono-chronic vs. poly-chronic	This cultural dimension portrays an understanding of time. In monochronic cultures, the individual steps required for a work process are carried out in sequence. Keeping to a schedule is very important; completing tasks is more important than cultivating relationships. In polychronic cultures, it is more usual to carry out several activities simultaneously. A schedule is not necessarily binding. Maintaining contacts has priority.
Speed of infor-mation	This cultural dimension expresses the preference for information according to the various speeds that processing requires and depending on the culture. This is mirrored in the headlines of daily newspapers. In cultures with a high speed of information headlines dominate that can be processed quickly but are less meaningful. On the other hand, in cultures with a lower speed of information, headlines dominate that do not need to be processed so quickly but are more meaningful instead.

Cultural dimensions according to Hall

Hofstede shows that national cultures and intranational sub-cultures exercise a considerable influence on the behavior of corporations, especially on their organization and management. To do this he uses the following six cultural dimensions (i.e. dimensions of national culture): power distance, individualism versus collectivism, masculinity versus femininity, uncertainty avoidance, long-term orientation, and indulgence versus restraint.

Cultural Dimension	Definition
Power Distance (= PDI)	The PD index indicates to what extent less powerful individuals accept and expect an unequal distribution of power. High power distance means that power is unequally distributed; low power distance means that power is more equally distributed.
Individualism (IDV)	In societies with a high IDV index the rights of the individual are particularly protected: self-determination, experience of the self and personal responsibility are important. In contrast, in a collectivist culture with a low IDV index integration into any kind of network dominates. The "we-feeling" is much more characteristic for such a culture.
Masculinity (MAS)	Hofstede considers feminine values to be solicitude, collaboration and modesty whereas masculine values are a readiness to compete and self-confidence. A high MAS index indicates that "typically masculine" values dominate; a low MAS index indicates that "typically feminine" values dominate.
Uncertainty Avoidance (UAI)	The key question of the UAI is: How great is the aversion to unforeseen situations? In this case the UAI does not correspond to risk avoidance! Cultures with a high UAI that want to avoid uncertainty are characterized by many established laws, guidelines and safety measures.
Long-term orientation (LTO)	This index indicates the length of the planning horizon in a society. Some of the values of members of an organization who focus on the long term are thriftiness and persistence; if they focus on the short term they tend to value flexibility and selfishness.
Indulgence vs. restraint (IVR)	Indulgence is indicative of a society that allows a relatively free gratification of basic, natural needs with respect to fun and enjoyment. Restraint is indicative of a society that suppresses the gratification of needs by means of strict social standards.

Cultural dimensions according to Hofstede

Fons Trompenaars is a Dutch management consultant and one of Hofstede's students. In his cultural model based on a data base of about 55,000 managers he has identified seven cultural dimensions: universalism versus particularism, individualism versus collectivism, affectivity versus neutrality, specificity versus diffuseness, achievement versus ascription, time orientation, and the relation to nature.

Cultural Dimension	Description
Universalism vs. particularism	*What are more important – rules or relationships?* This dimension portrays how people judge the behavior of others. A universalist prefers behavior based on rules in which the same rules apply everywhere and to everyone, independent of the situation and the personal relationship. A particularist tends to evaluate behavior in terms of the individual situation and the personal background of the person.
Individualism vs. collectivism	*Do we function in a group or as an individual?* In individualist cultures every single person tries to achieve personal objectives. His understanding of a family is the core family with parents and children. People in collectivist cultures think more in terms of (family) networks. Their own objectives are subordinate to the group from whom they expect support in difficult situations.
Affectivity vs. neutrality	*Do we show emotions?* In a neutral culture, feelings are kept under control or are not shown according to the dictates of convention. That does not mean that people in this culture are cold or suppress their feelings. They simply do not show their feelings openly. In affective cultures people show their feelings openly in facial expressions, gestures, volume level and choice of words.
Specificity vs. diffuseness	*How fully do we participate in public life?* In a specific culture, a business relationship is regulated by means of a contract. In a diffuse culture, the element of personal trust is added. In diffuse cultures the sight of the big picture and the relation of the individual elements to each other dominate. In specific cultures the problem is subdivided and individual solutions to the sub-projects are sought.
Achievement vs. ascription	*Do people gain their social status or professional position on their own merits?* In achievement-oriented cultures respect for executives is based on achievements (skills and knowledge). Decisions – no matter by whom – can be called into question with rational arguments. In contrast, respect in ascriptive societies is based on seniority, hierarchy or belonging to a social group (for example, family, religion, caste).
Time orientation	*Do we do things simultaneously (parallelism) or in sequence (seriality)?* In the latter case, the maxim "Time is Money" is paramount. It is valuable, limited and is used efficiently. On account of this, values like punctuality both in the private and professional sphere are rated as positive. A parallel understanding of time is also known by the terms "mañana" or "bukra" (sometime in the future). People from these cultures always keep several "balls in the air". They are flexible and can change from one topic to any number of others. In this case punctuality is less important than changing priorities that can sometimes lead to huge alterations to schedules. However, time in these cultures is also rated highly. Taking time for a relationship or business shows how important these are.

Cultural Dimension	Description
Relation to nature	*Do we try to control our environment or do we work in collaboration with it?* Many cultures believe they can influence and control their own fate by dint of their own actions. Other cultures tend to perceive themselves as part of nature and of a society that influences and restricts their actions to a great extent. They believe more in fate. Thus the Japanese always desire to live in harmony with their environment. For example, Japanese wear headphones or a face mask so as not to disturb or infect other people. In contrast, Americans do not want to be disturbed by the environment or infected by other people.

Cultural dimensions according to Trompenaars

In addition, Trompenaars also draws a distinction between a work culture and a leisure culture. The former contains values that are characterized by the environment (for example: How does one act in a team? How does one achieve objectives?). The latter portrays behavior in dealing with friends and family and behavior in solving private problems. Both of these can be quite different as is evident in the example of employees of a multi-national corporation in a developing country. In the office they cope with their jobs using the latest technology and management methods in a corporate culture that is American-biased whereas at home they live according to the customs and rituals of their ancient culture. That is not a contradiction but a reality that can be met with more and more frequently.

The GLOBE Project

The GLOBE project established by sociologist Robert J. House has a data base of about 17,000 managers. Their data were collected in the period between 1994 and 1997 and are used by various sociologists carrying out research in the field of intercultural leadership. The findings are based on nine cultural dimensions: power distance, uncertainty avoidance, institutional collectivism, in-group collectivism, assertiveness, gender egalitarianism, future orientation, humane orientation and performance orientation. Some of this methodology was adopted by Hofstede and – despite criticism by him – has confirmed his own results to a large extent.

World Value Survey (WVS)

The WVS is a study to measure values and beliefs and is carried out on a regular basis. It also examines how these change and which impact they have on politics and society. In the meantime, the data collection compromises 360 items that have been collected in more than 100 countries. This makes it the most comprehensive, freely available data bank on intercultural management. Using the WVS it was possible to prove conclusively the impact of people's beliefs on economic development. The WVS is carried out by the non-profit making World Values Survey Association in Stockholm, Sweden. The association was founded in 1981.

There are considerable differences in the cultural dimensions of all the cultural models depicted here. They partly use identical terms which are, however, interpreted differently. Moreover, the results are based on different data. To the chagrin of the practical user, they afford no unequivocal conditional statements (if A, then B) and no comprehensive explanatory model. Besides, the actual behavior varies according to the context. Nevertheless, all the cultural models provide valuable approaches from different points of view, which sensitize the global manager to intercultural challenges. Today the WVS provides all researchers and practitioners with a high-quality data bank for their own research and use. Thus, in conjunction with Dülfer's Layer Model, the global manager has a comprehensive collection of material on other cultures.

All the cultural models described have one thing in common – the fact that cultures only exist in comparison with each other. The values achieved are relative and only gain significance when they are compared with those of other cultures. The relevant findings could be confirmed in diverse studies – that is they have remained stable over a long period. Thus national cultures tend to change extremely slowly and together. The following sections concentrate entirely on work culture.

3.3. Differences between National Cultures

The starting point for measuring the differences between two cultures is always one's own culture. This presupposes that one is aware of one's own culture. Chinese employees will only understand the difference between their own culture and that of an American if they understand their own culture with its typical values, beliefs and behavior.

It becomes complicated if an Indian works for an English corporation in Dubai and manages an international project team of employees from various cultures. But that is something for later in the chapter. First of all it will be shown how the cultural distance between two cultures is measured. Some of the differences between the two cultures are illustrated by means of an example. The results form a basis for creating a cultural profile.

"In an ideal world a policeman would be English, a car mechanic German, a cook French, a lover Italian and everything would be organized by a Swiss national. It would be less ideal if the policeman were German, the car mechanic French, the cook English, the lover Swiss and everything was organized by an Italian."

This well-known comparison shows the meaning of stereotypes, clichés and prejudices. At the same time, attributes are closely linked to nations and are based on the assumed strengths and weaknesses of the individual countries. They form an interesting starting point for interpreting cultural differences but are no replacement for the following comprehensive analysis.

Let us, for examples, compare Germans with Italians and Japanese. By means of Geert Hofstede's cultural dimensions explained above and used as an example we arrive at the results shown in Table 10.

Cultural Dimension	Italians	Germans	Diff. It-Ge	Japanese	Diff. Jp-Ge
PDI Power distance	50	35	15	54	19
UAI Uncertainty avoidance	75	65	10	92	27
MAS Masculinity	70	66	4	95	29
IDV Individualism	76	67	9	46	21
LTO Long term orientation	33	31	2	75	44
Cultural distance	-	-	40		140

Table10: Cultural dimensions according to Hofstede in a comparison between countries
Source: http://geert-hofstede.com/countries.html

The table shows values for two cultures. However, it should be noted that statements about cultures never reflect reality but are always relative and general and only attain their value through the difference that is determined between them.

The cultural distance between Italians and Germans is 40. The cultural distance defines the sum of all the deviations whether positive or negative. The value 40 is again relative. It only becomes significant in a comparison with another cultural distance, for example between Japanese and Germans. At 140 this is perceptibly higher than the distance between Germans and Italians. Nevertheless, there is also a perceptible difference between the last two cultures. In our example, all the cultural dimensions are weighted equally. Depending on the organization observed and the formulation of the questions, the weighting of individual dimensions can deviate. Moreover, a qualitative statement based on a quantitative analysis ought to be scrutinized with the utmost care.

Cultural distance can be used as criteria for choosing the market entry form. Even if the conditions were the same, a German entrepreneur would choose a more risky form for market entry into Italy (for example: a subsidiary of his own) than for market entry into Japan where he might choose a local partner for market entry to bridge the cultural distance (for example: joint venture).

Let us have a look at the cultural dimensions in detail (see Table 11). The greatest differences between Germans and Italians are to be found in the cultural dimensions power distance, uncertainty avoidance and individualism. The other two dimensions show relatively slight differences from a quantitative point of view. Basically deviations of ten points and more are regarded as significant. For that reason, not all cultural dimensions are examined in the analysis of the cultural difference between Germany and Italy.

However, this does not automatically mean that from a qualitative point of view there are no differences. In a manner of speaking, there can be relevant differences especially in connection with other cultural dimensions. This can certainly be confirmed by any German or Italian familiar with each other's culture using a large number of examples. In contrast all the cultural dimensions between Germans and Japanese exhibit perceptible differences.

In the following step, three cultural dimensions with the greatest cultural distance are looked at in detail. The differences are highlighted and possible relations between the individual cultural dimensions are investigated.

Cultural dimension (according to Hofstede)	Italians	Germans
PDI Power distance *(Difference 15)*	• Italy has medium power distance. • Hierarchy and privileges arising thereof are accepted. • Seniority is a criterion for eligibility for the next step in a career. • Status symbols express power and hierarchy.	• Germany has low power distance. • High decentralization and strong middle class (many SMEs). • Management characterized by strong co-determination, decision-making in committees and a participative and direct leadership style with little direct control. • Acceptance of executives on the basis of expertise and the example they set.
UAI Uncertainty avoidance *(Difference 10)*	• Italians avoid uncertainty as far as possible. • Italy has a multitude of laws and rules and very pronounced bureaucracy which Italians handle with great "creativity".	• Germans avoid uncertainty. • This is illustrated in the legal system which sets structural limits but also regulates many details.
IND Individualism *(Difference 9)*	• Italy is an individualistic, ego-centered society (especially in the north). • Loyalty exists mainly to one's own objectives and ideas which in cases of doubt are given priority.	• Germany is an individualistic society. • Loyalty to the nuclear family and the company based on feelings of duty and responsibility. • Communication is direct.
Connection UAI / PDI	**High values in UAI and PDI mean a combination of central decision-making and formalized decision-making and control processes.**	**A high UAI with low PDI mean that safety through expertise, precise rules at strategic level and in the definition of details are valued.**

Table 11: Individual analysis of cultural dimensions according to Hofstede

The two cultural dimensions "uncertainty avoidance" and "power distance" are very important when creating a cultural profile. Accordingly, organizations in Italy are usually very bureaucratic and hierarchic, and decision-making is centralized. This tendency is aggravated even more by crises. The management of such organizations presents both Italians and all foreigners with a huge challenge. Italians react by paying strict attention to which rules have to be followed and when; moreover, they also reach their desired objective via their network. Germans, too, try to regulate and plan everything to the last detail. Unlike the Italians they want to push through the planned objectives with all their might and in doing so they set almost inhuman moral standards for themselves. Italians react more strongly to external influences in their implementation and are more flexible in adapting solutions, objectives and activities.

Analyzing the relations between two or more cultural dimensions can provide additional information. Therefore, a high level of the cultural dimensions "power distance", "uncertainty avoidance" and "individualism" indicate possible tensions between hierarchic, centralized organizations with very formalized processes on the one hand and the strong need for self-fulfillment on the other hand. This results in highly differentiated organization charts, for example. Many Italians find their niche in these with an attractive title and making a good impression (key word: "bella figura").

Trompenaars' and Hall's cultural dimensions provide further examples of cultural differences between Italians and Germans. The four cultural dimensions portrayed in Table 12 again show perceptible cultural differences that are crucial for creating a cultural profile.

The evaluation of cultural differences is always neutral and respectful. However, it is not only the measurements of the specific cultural dimensions obtained that are analyzed; the relations between various cultural dimensions are analyzed, too. However the evaluation never interprets or judges a culture or culture-specific behavior. Compiling cultural differences requires a great deal of experience so that these do not end up as speculation, interpretation, judgments, stereotypes or clichés.

Cultural dimension (according to Trompenaars and Hall)	Italians	Germans
Universalism versus particularism	**Particularism** • Apart from laws and rules, the individual situation and the relation to the people affected are also important to Italians.	**Universalism** • For Germans, laws and rules are almost superhuman. These are given priority over relations.
Time orientation	**Polychronic** • Italians carry out several tasks simultaneously. That way they can bridge waiting periods flexibly. • North Italians in particular are punctual in a professional context. This can be different in the private sphere.	**Monochronic** • Germans carry out tasks one after the other and try to keep appointments as arranged. • Germans usually bridge waiting periods by simply waiting or killing time.
Spatial awareness and corporeality	**High contact** • HC cultures stand closer to each other. • HC cultures tend to use physical contact in conversations or in greetings.	**Low contact** • LC cultures maintain greater physical distance. • LC cultures restrict physical contact to a handshake when greeting. • Physical contact during a conversation is highly unusual.
Context orientation	**High context** • Strongly implicit communication through close long-term relations. • Private and professional overlapping.	**Low context** • Strongly explicit communication which means that instructions must be unequivocal and easy to understand because the context is missing. • Due to different roles in professional and private life and frequent job changes, misunderstandings can often arise if there is no clear communication.
Combination of time and context orientation	**Often a higher proportion of leisure time but also overlapping of professional and private interests (keyword: "work to live").**	**Work is strictly separated from private life. Considerable amount of time invested in work (keyword: "live to work").**

Table 12: Cultural dimensions according to Trompenaars and Hall

This method for measuring cultural distance and interpreting cultural differences enables the global manager to obtain suitable guidance at a glance. The method introduced here is the simplest approach available. It gives examples of how to recognize and define cultural differences.

In measuring and defining cultural differences only two cultures are compared with each other. The basis is always one's own national culture or the corporate culture. The cultural differences in the specific cultural dimensions provide the cultural distance and show where the most significant deviations exist between the two cultures under review.

It is advisable to examine the cultural dimensions of all available cultural models for cultural differences. The quality of the results depends to a large extent on a structured and professional approach. Too much imagination and creativity will mean that objectives will not be reached. For that reason only employees with appropriate experience and training should be entrusted with creating cultural profiles.

3.4. Creating a Cultural Profile

Cultural profiles are a valuable tool for global managers. Not only do cultural profiles provide general information about a country and its people as well as useful tips for the daily life of a global manager in this cultural field, they also specify the demands made on the behavior of international executives towards local employees. These include for example communication, managing and motivating employees and establishing organizations and relationships.

A cultural profile includes the major cultural differences and aims at promoting sensitivity in the global manager. Consequently, cultural profiles are short and to the point and can be used easily and quickly as required and can be supplemented according to specific requirements. Intercultural training in dealing with cultural profiles beforehand increases efficiency perceptibly.

Cultural profiles are always written from the point of view of a specific culture: either that of the global manager, the corporate culture or the national culture of corporate headquarters. Cultural profiles are always created for a single culture – the culture of the target country. The objective of the cultural profile is to improve dealings with local employees and other stakeholders.

Cultural profiles can be individualized easily by supplementing them with company-specific elements: for example codes of behavior in critical situations (for example: corruption and crises), dealing with corporate culture) or obligations to notify the authorities in high-risk countries.

A cultural profile can now be created using the cultural differences that have been mentioned. In practice this contains the relevant differences in everyday dealings between both cultures that could be a challenge to a global manager. These cultural profiles are designed in such a way that every global manager, employee who has dealings with companies abroad or a service technician with no precise knowledge of the country or culture receives valuable tips and recommendations for action that will make it easier to carry out tasks. Cultural profiles have proved particularly valuable for employees who travel to various countries or only have occasional contact to foreign subsidiaries (for example: auditing, financial controlling, and marketing).

Fig. 34: Possible elements of a cultural profile

Fig. 34 gives an example of the elements that might be included in cultural profiles. The eight cultural elements given cover most aspects of a cultural profile. However, the number of elements depends on the requirements of the company or the international organization. Thus specific cultural elements such as corporate culture or ways of behaving in critical situations or in crisis can be added.

The individual cultural elements are depicted in Table 13. This is followed by examples providing details of some cultural elements in order to emphasize the benefit of cultural profiles especially for the everyday work of the global manager. The results of the individual cultural elements are based on data banks such as the World Value Survey, the careful analysis of available research results, my own research and the well-known cultural dimensions by Hofstede, Trompenaars, Hall and others. Moreover, every user has the opportunity to supplement his specific experiences. The latter is particularly to be recommended because cultural profiles thus support organizations in developing their own intercultural competence.

Elements of cultural profiles	Definition
Design of organizational structure	Symbols, rituals and heroes define an organizational culture. Thus, every organization defines its own culture, starting with the significance of hierarchies to the description of jobs and to the necessity of formal/ bureaucratic processes. Another element is the extent to which tasks, competences and responsibility are delegated/decentralized or centralized.
Decision making	In many cultures employees want to assume responsibility, make decisions themselves or at least prepare the groundwork for these. In other cultures employees prefer to concentrate on their work and expect to be given clear guidelines on time, budgets and work content.
Leadership	Leadership culture can be authoritarian or participative whereby authority can rest with a single person or with a group such as a family. It influences the number of levels in the hierarchy and the decision-making processes in an organization. The leadership culture determines and influences all the cultural elements.
Motivation and incentive schemes	This describes which incentives motivate employees. In some countries security and stability are to the fore while in other countries flexibility, acceptance of responsibility and a willingness to take risks are held in high regard. This has an impact on career and remuneration schemes where a distinction is made between the objectives, incentives and bonuses of the individual and the group.

Elements of cultural profiles	Definition
Communicational behavior	Interpersonal communication has verbal and non-verbal components. Communication in organizations is based on the corporate culture, e.g. with regard to spatial awareness and time orientation.
Relationships	Here the focus is on the distinction between a culture oriented towards relationships or towards facts; and on the way of conducting business and decision-making in a country.
Specification of corporate objectives	The definition of corporate objectives and the personal objectives of the individual employee is shaped to a large extent by the national culture in question. For that reason short-term growth targets dominate in Anglo-Saxon countries whereas other cultures place more emphasis on sustainability.
Information about the country	This provides business travelers with data from politics, business, the infrastructure and society and important addresses to contact.
Travel tips	These provide business travelers with tips on behavior at typical events such as meals, welcoming people, procedures at meetings and overnight stays, travel and communication

Table 13: Examples of elements of cultural profiles

Element 1: Design of the Organizational Structure – Structure follows Strategy and Culture

In designing the organizational structure the global manager faces a conflict of objectives. On the one hand, the local subsidiary has to take the local culture and all other local framework conditions into account and on the other hand these have to be integrated into the entire corporation. This is a challenging task. Local managers have to learn to meet the expectations of an international proprietor and the demands of the local market. The managers from headquarters who sit on the supervisory boards of the local subsidiary need to learn how to get their bearings in a local organizational structure and to focus on the local culture.

The cultural dimension "power distance" is very pronounced in Italian culture. Organization is hierarchical; leadership style is authoritarian; decision-making is centralized and employees expect clear decisions and guidelines.

The cultural dimension "uncertainty avoidance" also has a high value in the Italian culture. The management of the organization is very formal and bureaucratic. The economy and the labor market are strictly regulated. There are comprehensive process and job descriptions and a multitude of controlling and auditing bodies. Although many laws are contradictory, bureaucracy conveys a feeling of security. However, it is less a matter of keeping rules, implementing plans successfully or achieving all the targets. It is by dint of its very existence that bureaucracy creates security.

Managing Italian subsidiaries is very labor-intensive for German global managers. For a start they have to battle their way through a complex bureaucracy that requires a great deal of time to prepare the necessary documents. Then they need time to manage the organization as they have to provide clear guidelines for operations and assume responsibility for minor decisions, too. Moreover, the management structures are complex, too. An Italian board of directors has more competences and more responsibility, too, than a German supervisory board. In addition to the chairman there is also a delegate to the board of directors, which is similar to the general manager; the director can be compared with a managing director. Finding the right structure is a huge challenge for global managers, who only know the general manager of a German GmbH (equivalent of a limited liability company).

Apart from the challenges presented by a formal structure global managers – especially with regards to the integration of acquired Italian corporations – have to take the informal organization (cordata) into account. As is the case in other cultures, this is crucial for the successful functioning of an organization. As Italians like to work with people they know and they set great store by the family, these networks are based on long-standing relationships and dependencies. As a result, relatives and members of the families in the network are often given preference when new positions have to be filled. Like everything else, this has its advantages and disadvantages. Although it means that it is not always the best qualified employee who is given the position, the family assumes responsibility for the success of the hiring.

A further challenge is the role played by the global managers. Usually they are not members of the management board and quite often they are not on the supervisory board of the subsidiary which normally includes the Head of Legal Services, the Head of Finance and a member of the Group executive board. In cultures with high power distance that attach great importance to titles and hierarchy, executives will only work with a global manager who has the same standing in the hierarchy. This is something that Germans corporations find it difficult to understand in most cases. From the viewpoint of the local management, global managers are little more than glorified assistants or travel directors if the principle of seniority is ignored, privileges and status symbols are missing and they have no formal function. In such instances, the heads of the overseas subsidiaries will always have to refer to the "patriarchs". However, from the point of view of headquarters the global managers are the project managers in charge. These different points of view reduce the global manager's efficiency enormously.

The position of the local management is difficult, too. It is accustomed to receiving clear instructions from a "patriarch" who has the privileges, status symbols and decision-making authority. Now in addition to the global manager there are both the Board members from the various departments and the corporate management that does not have much time and therefore is not in a position to meet the implicit expectations of the local management even in a limited way. There are no clear statements to be had from either side. This insecurity results in a leadership vacuum. Practice shows that this leadership vacuum is usually not recognized despite considerable friction losses. As a rule one makes do with exchanging the local managing director. In this case it is best to hire a local managing director from the target country, who has management experience in both cultures and is, therefore, in a position to build a bridge between the two cultures.

No doubt the interested reader now expects a few comments on the subject of time orientation and punctuality in particular. It is said of Germans that they are always punctual. This is even expected of them. Because of this, I have always found Italians to be very punctual especially with regard to their jobs. They frequently adapt to the Germans and they were very surprised when I once arrived later. Due to the lack of infrastructure in the country, it is often difficult for people to keep appointments despite good planning. It is always a good idea to take some work with you. That should not present a problem in the present-day technical era.

Element 2: Decision Making

The question on the concentration of decision-making power is answered for example by the cultural dimension "power distance". In cultures with high PDI decisions tend to be taken centrally, whereas in cultures with low PDI there is a tendency for decisions to be taken decentrally and for employees to be integrated into decision making processes. Therefore, the decision-making processes also reflect the organizational structure (compare Element 1).

The cultural dimension "uncertainty avoidance" defines among other things the structuring of activities as well as formal rules and process descriptions (example: decision-making processes). Thus cultures with high uncertainty avoidance incline towards a vast number of formal processes and regulations.

The combination of the two cultural dimensions mentioned above is of particular interest. In cultures, therefore, with relatively low PDI and distinctive UAI, decision-making is gladly delegated to formal processes. As in Germany, for example, there is more trust in rules or machines than in people.

In cultures with rather high PDI and distinctive UAI, corporations are managed by formal and strictly hierarchical decision-making processes.

Employees from a culture where the cultural dimension "uncertainty avoidance" is very pronounced expect certain skills from global managers independent of their origins; they expect among other things the ability:

- to take decisions clearly and precisely,
- to define guidelines for operations (priority, time, resources, objectives),
- to avoid conflicts and diverging opinions in the organization (as far as possible),
- to provide (allegedly) detailed arrangements for controlling the future (business plan) and
- to introduce formal and standardized decision-making processes.

The fact that the cultural dimension "power distance" is very pronounced requires German global managers to clearly define and differentiate the individual functions with the various tasks, competences and responsibilities within their organizations. At the same time the employees in higher positions are expected to be given privileges and status symbols.

For an organization to function efficiently, global managers also rely on the informal organization (cordata) of long-standing relationships and dependencies. Integration is certainly difficult but if it succeeds, it is very useful.

Diplomatically experienced global managers who are used to working on a task-oriented rather than a relationship-oriented basis face a considerable challenge. When they ask employees: "How would you decide?" most of them do not understand and reply: "Why ask me? That's not my job. That's not what I'm paid for." This is interpreted as weakness on the part of global managers. They lose their reputation as leaders and the organization loses efficiency because there are no clear guidelines.

Element 3: Leadership

In any culture, the relationship between superiors and their subordinates is based on common values. Leadership style and techniques are therefore dependent on the national culture or the distinct characteristics of the various cultural dimensions.

In feminine cultures like the Netherlands executives are rather modest and solve problems intuitively, they prefer to achieve a consensus (Polder Model) and set great store by close collaboration. In masculine, individualistic cultures like the Anglo-Saxon countries successful executives are looked up to as heroes. Asian cultures that have a high LTO attach great importance to securing the existence of the corporations in the long term and to a sustainable expansion of their market share. Moreover, the low IDV value shows that Chinese family-owned companies are very family-oriented.

In addition to culture the local framework conditions (for example: education) are a key factor in managing employees. It can frequently happen that a young Italian employee has a university degree but very rarely does he have traditional, professional training. Despite the best prerequisites at the cognitive level, practical skills and (especially in the case of university graduates) job experience are often missing. Moreover, such young people are usually hard-working, committed, ambitious and creative but due to the high power distance seldom show much initiative. The superior, the global manager, is required, especially at the beginning of working together, to channel these skills by managing according to the guidelines for operations, by controlling results, by supporting the employee in the implementation of tasks and by making clear decisions. This way the employee gains security and the close collaboration allows a personal relationship to develop.

A global manager has to place emphasis on realistic planning and meeting the stipulated objectives. On account of the considerable inclination towards uncertainty avoidance, Italian employees value precise planning but they feel less tied to planning than Central or Northern Europeans, for example. They try to achieve these but react to external and internal influences more flexibly.

The fact that cultural "individualism" is very pronounced means that Italians put strong emphasis on themselves and their own careers. In this case, a global manager can work well with individual objectives as well as monetary and non-monetary incentives. Status symbols and privileges that help employees to make a "bella figura" in their environment are particularly popular.

The Italian economy is characterized by very successful owner-managed small and medium-sized companies. In these companies the patriarch (alone or with other family members) makes all the decisions. The employees adapt to this centralized decision making and in the course of many years of collaboration a close mutual trust develops. In this culture there are few employees with the training to work in a matrix organization and that is what large multi-national corporations prefer.

Polychronic time orientation ought to be taken into consideration when planning meetings. Although employees appear punctually at meetings, they go away immediately to deal with something else if not all the participants are present. During meetings, they discuss and phone at the same time. This makes co-ordination difficult for the global manager but the employees are, however, very flexible. They can carry out several tasks at once and they react to external changes very quickly. This example of monochronic and polychronic time orientation – i.e. of co-ordination and flexibility – shows clearly that connecting various skills symbiotically is more sensible than forging unsatisfactory compromises. However, for this to work the global manager needs to explain the cultural differences to the employees, to demonstrate the advantages of both cultures and thus help them to learn the respective skills of each other.

Element 4: Motivation and Incentive Schemes

Employees' motivation is based on their culture. Typical incentives are remuneration, status and recognition, and work content and career prospects. Incentive schemes need to be geared to the specific culture because values and beliefs differ with respect to work, society and one's own life. Employees from cultures with high uncertainty avoidance are more geared to security and stability. The prospect of a secure job and a stable environment provides them with a considerable incentive. The reaction to crises is to have even more bureaucracy and government in order to be able to have the future under control. Remuneration is based more on seniority and titles than on performance. The majority of Italian university graduates thus prefers to work for the government. In contrast, employees from cultures with low uncertainty avoidance tend to be more open to performance-oriented remuneration, constant change and corporate responsibility. Business models that are subject to quick change and rely on innovations are more likely to be found in cultures with low uncertainty avoidance. For that reason, technology companies are mainly located in these cultures. Consequently, many university graduates in the US prefer to work for start-up companies.

Employees from cultures with high power distance can be motivated by good relations with their immediate superiors. Employees from cultures with low power distance gain motivation from a delegation of responsibility, work in autonomous (project) teams and the exchange of ideas with colleagues or additional benefits such as childcare and a canteen.

Employees from cultures with high individualism can be motivated by personal recognition (for example: the employee of the month), being able to work independently and individual incentives such as bonuses, stock options and career perspectives. Employees from cultures with high collectivism gain their motivation mainly from working in a group, clear objectives and a group bonus as a reward. Highlighting an individual member of the group is more likely to be unsettling because it upsets the harmony of the group.

Employees from cultures with high masculinity are more easily motivated by traditional roles, strict separation of professional and private life as well as performance-based compensation at all levels of the hierarchy. Employees from cultures with high femininity can be motivated by modern working practices where they can combine profession and family (for example: flexible working hours and working from home).

This example shows that our German global managers can motivate their Italian employees by offering long-term job-security, a lasting positive working relationship built on trust paired with individual incentives and personal recognition in the form of privileges and status symbols in a traditional working environment. Status symbols and titles in particular are very important to Italian employees as can be observed in the much differentiated organization with its manifold functions.

A cultural profile depicts the motivators that are specific to the culture and gives tips for practical implementation.

Element 5: Communicational Behavior

Communicational behavior in person-to-person talks and group discussions depends very much on the specific culture. It not only comprises verbal communication but also non-verbal elements such as facial expressions, gestures, proximity, context, spatial awareness, and dealing with pauses in speech and volume. Cultures also communicate via architecture, clothing, status symbols or appearance. Most communication is non-verbal.

Depending on the culture, communication can be geared towards facts or relationships. The distinction can also depend on the various stages of the conversation or talks. In many cultures, therefore, the aim of communication at the beginning of talks or at a meal together is to build up trust or a personal relationship before getting down to business.

A further dimension that needs to be taken into consideration is the context. In so-called "high-context" cultures conversation partners only need a few words to understand the content of a conversation. Understanding comes from the context and non-verbal communication. "Low-context" cultures are characterized by a strict separation of private and professional roles and therefore the conversation partners do not know the contexts. They do not have the necessary background information. Consequently the verbal communication has to provide a large amount of additional information.

A further level of communication is spatial awareness: the distance between people while they are communicating. In principle, collectivist cultures are more likely to be contact cultures. The space between the members is much narrower, they embrace each other in greeting and saying farewell and there is a certain physical contact (for example: backslapping) during conversations. In individualistic cultures it is the exact opposite.

In communication, typical Italians show their feelings in gestures, facial expressions, and the volume level of speech and choice of words and expect a similar reaction from their conversation partners. If these are Germans, they are likely to be disappointed for the Germans are more likely to have the impression that talks are escalating and will try to calm things down. They wish to remove the emotions from the talks and concentrate on facts. As a result they both talk at cross purposes and the objective of the talks is not achieved. For that reason, global managers would be better to have an experienced and highly qualified interpreter present at crucial talks because an interpreter translates both verbal and non-verbal content and bridges the cultural differences.

A further element of communication is the so-called "reporting lines" in international corporations. One of a global manager's tasks is integrating new companies into the structure of the global company. Conflicts can arise due to diverse communication and information cultures. In cultures with high power distance (authoritarian and centralized), external communication (even within the global company) is always via the "patriarch" at the top of the pyramid. In cultures with low power distance (participative and decentralized) the individual departments are globally networked and communicate with each other within the terms of their responsibility. Conflicts are inevitable in this constellation. If the "patriarch" is bypassed, employees are uncertain what to do. In most cases they will not react to a request to report. This problem can only be solved by assigning the reporting to the employee in the department and coordinating the contents with the "patriarch" before the report is sent off.

A cultural profile records the major rules of communication between two cultures. This enables all those participating in talks to avoid major errors in communication and ensures an efficient exchange of information whereby the communication content is also a key factor. When establishing a relationship or during a business meal, Italians like to talk about history, literature, art and life style. The latter includes fashion, food and drink. As a rule, Italians have a high standard of general education. In comparison many global managers will quickly reach their limits.

Cultural profiles are a powerful, efficient, flexible work instrument for global managers and all employees with contacts abroad and it is easy to use. It provides the desired results immediately as required.

Cultural profiles help to develop an awareness of cultural differences. A global manager ought not to avoid a discussion on the impact of cultural differences on the performance of teams but needs to deliberately initiate this. It is only within the framework of a frank discussion that mutual trust can be established and belief in the project objectives strengthened.

Cultural profiles are multi-dimensional. They show the relationships between the individual cultural elements; they formulate the tips for behavior in simple language and help to establish a deeper understanding of the other culture.

Cultural differences can only be solved if the background to these is known. However, it is not just a matter of understanding the various behavior patterns; it is also a question of knowing their origins and learning from them. Moreover, it is not a question of whether the behavior is "right" or "wrong"; the only thing of interest is the assumptions underlying them. This is what a cultural profile offers. It is therefore a tool for everyday use. A team can only move at this level and remain there if there is more openness and common effort. If this succeeds, it provides a clear competitive edge.

Successful executives make use of cultural differences and combine the best of both worlds. It is a matter of combining the strengths of the two cultures – i.e. the synergies and symbioses – instead of reaching compromises which usually only permit average solutions.

3.5. Dimensions of Organizational Cultures

The question as to the significance of organizational culture compared with the respective national cultures plays a major role especially in the case of MNEs. Although this topic is often governed by emotions and observers suspect cultural conflicts everywhere, the opposite is the case. In an MNE employees with very different national cultures work on common objectives. The more efficiently, the more respectfully, the more smoothly and the more synergistically collaboration is the more successful the MNE will be. This requires a strong organizational culture that is respected by all of the employees: Moreover their individual strengths will show to advantage.

While employees from very different national cultures work successfully in an MNE during the day, they live with their families in the traditions of their respective local culture after work. Although this might appear to be a contradiction, it shows the ability of people to adapt their behavior to specific requirements without forsaking their own values and beliefs. It also proves the ability of organizational cultures to integrate employees of very different backgrounds into the analogical melting pot and to make synergistic use of their respective strengths.

This section shows which instruments can be used by global managers to be successful in the management of intercultural teams in a global environment.

Organizational Cultures Compared to National Cultures

There is a perceptible difference between an organizational culture and a national culture. The values and beliefs of a national culture are learned from one's own family, friends and teachers in childhood. Employees do not learn an organizational culture – independent of their own national culture – until they are adults and take up a position in the company – i.e. when their system of values already exists.

Every form of organization has its own culture. Therefore the organizational culture particularly of international organizations like NGOs, MNEs, UNO or the IOC is capable of integrating employees and stakeholders from the most diverse national cultures without calling their values and beliefs into question. This works only because superficial organizational practices are involved which unlike values and beliefs are easier to adapt to new challenges.

National cultures – like organizational cultures and their practices – provide their own specific institutions. Thus, administration, business, schools, media, science, law and art are a reflection of a culture whereby each culture regulates life in the community according to its own requirements.

Practices differ with regards to symbols, rituals and heroes. The latter denotes the implicit prerequisites for a career in an organization. If all the board members are engineers, a historian's chances are slim. Symbols such as a dress code, the size of the office and company car and titles are directed outwards and are only understood by insiders. Rituals are regularly recurring actions. Good examples of these are financial planning and control and the often legendary Christmas party.

The culture of every organization and its practices is shaped by the national culture of the country of its origin. This also applies to rituals like financial planning and control that in the case of internationalization are usually exported to the respective national culture without adaptation. Planning means that insecurity is reduced. Control means a wielding of power. On the one hand control is carried out impersonally by means of reporting systems and on the other hand it is personal when expatriates are posted abroad.

However, the structuring of financial planning and control also depends on the national culture of the country of origin. In masculine cultures figures are more to the fore than in feminine cultures. The planning horizon is influenced by the LTO of a national culture. In collectivist, high-context cultures figures are rarely used as a basis for a decision. Consequently the status of bookkeepers and lawyers is lower there.

The well-known study by the IRIC (Institute for Research on Intercultural Cooperation) attempted to define organizational culture in the same way as national cultures by using the six dimensions of perceived common practices but not of values. The dimensions are: pragmatic vs. normative, tight vs. loose control, open vs. closed system, professional vs. parochial, employee vs. job orientation, results vs. process orientation. The results are also used to identify subcultures. These are certainly dependent on the respective national cultures, but also on the function and the position in the hierarchy. Thus the organizational culture usually distinguishes between employees with a university degree in departments in headquarters and employees in production or in sales and customer service.

The HR department plays a major role in the development of the organizational culture. On the one hand, it pays attention to the cultural fit of applicants and on the other hand new employees are made familiar with the rituals of the organization during their initial training. This also includes the intercultural communication in an organization.

Exporting the organizational culture is particularly crucial in opening up new foreign markets regardless of the market entry form. In this case one expatriate is certainly enough to control a subsidiary. As such employees are usually alone; therefore, they will quickly become integrated into the national culture of the new foreign market. It is very different if a group of employees is posted abroad. These bring their organizational culture and all its practices with them and are therefore able to transfer them into the new subsidiary. Thus, integrating groups of employees is more difficult than integrating individuals.

Intercultural Management of Multi-National Organizations

The challenges in dealing with cultures can be demonstrated by the following example. A global pharmaceutical company with a distinctive international organizational culture has its headquarters and its main administration with R & D, production facilities and many other departments in Switzerland. More than 90 percent of its customers are in foreign markets. That also applies to the majority of the shareholders and employees in the top two management levels. The organizational culture is global. The legislation and the regulation that determine the framework conditions are shaped by the national culture of the headquarters. On the one hand the corporate management needs to maintain its global organizational culture to remain competitive and on the other hand it needs to respect the sensitivities of the local culture to maintain its freedom of action (keyword: good corporate citizen).

The second challenge in dealing with other cultures is HR policy. Within the framework of a geocentric personnel selection process, an American woman from the USA is rated as the candidate with the best qualifications and is appointed professor at an elite French university. On the one hand she will adapt her behavior to the organizational culture to be successful in her profession and on the other hand she will adapt to the national culture of her new domicile. Although this integration process presents the university with a huge challenge, there is the threat of additional conflicts with the national culture. Fears of foreign infiltration or anxiety about jobs can – if they are not taken seriously enough – quickly result in legislative initiatives that restrict the freedom of action of a globally-oriented organization and reduce its competitiveness. Although learning the French language is not necessary for integration into the organizational culture because research and teaching are in English, knowledge of French is an indispensible prerequisite for integration into the national culture.

The third challenge is the management of an intercultural organization. A new employee from Nigeria, for example, will meet colleagues from very different cultures at his new workplace. Successful collaboration will only work if the employees involved know their own culture and are capable of working with other national cultures using for example the mutually accepted practices and tools of the organizational culture. A further dimension is added if the new employee is posted to China temporarily to work on a project. In China he represents a global corporation – for example from the USA. His Chinese conversation partners now expect behavior from him, a Nigerian, which they associate with the national culture of the USA.

These simple examples clearly demonstrate the challenges presented by intercultural management. They are also evidence that it is not just the global manager that is expected to have a high intercultural competence. All employees today are expected to have it, too. Therefore, intercultural competence is clearly a prerequisite for success on international markets. This not only requires regular and intensive training but also the development of tools that lend employees efficient support in coping with everyday intercultural situations.

An organizational culture is frequently shaped by the homeland of the company. As diversity and internationalization increase this influence wanes but it never disappears entirely. This is not necessarily a disadvantage. In this way German car-makers and engineers, Japanese and Korean electronics companies, American social-media platforms and film

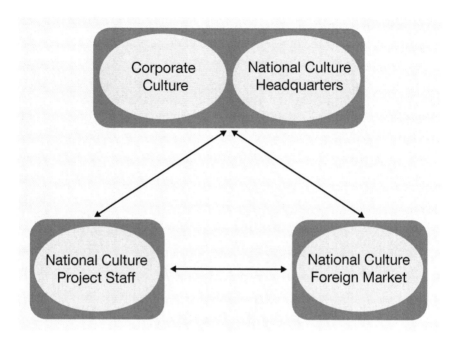

Fig. 35: Interaction of organizational cultures and national culture

studios or Italian and French fashion designers profit from the specific culture of their home markets. Porter refers to this as the "competitive advantage of nations". It can also change and have the opposite effect. By revealing his customers' data with almost unduly compliant haste a private Swiss banker forfeits the competitive advantage and basis for higher prices of his traditional discretion, reliability and the confidence placed in him. The same applies to the Japanese engineer of consumer electronics if, from the customers' point of view, the quality does not come up to expectation.

The main task of the global manager in the global network of an international corporation is maintaining the balance between adapting locally and integrating globally – i.e. successfully integrating apparently contradictory cultures into one huge entity. In other words, trying to find in all the diversity what can be united.

Realizing Synergies in Complex Multi-Cultural Situations

Multi-national corporations and global groups need a strong organizational culture that is global, targeted and open to other cultures and based to a large extent on the culture of the home market and the framework conditions prevailing there. On the one hand, an organizational culture comprises clear values with defined internal and external behavior patters and on the other hand it has the ability to integrate the most diverse national cultures into an analogical melting pot.

An intercultural and international organizational culture is based on the following assumptions:

* The decisive success factor in international management is the quality of the individual members of the project team.
* International management is always intercultural management, too.
* Geocentric personnel selection provides a corporation with the greatest possible access to qualified and talented employees independent of culture, age, sex and origin. As a result, intercultural teams are not only to be found in foreign departments.
* Self-reference criterion describes the unconscious evaluation of other behavior patterns against the background of one's own culture. It is crucial for employees to be aware of their own culture in order to recognize cultural differences and to be able to work with employees from other cultures.
* Professionalism: In cases of doubt, one's own experience and competences count for relatively little in other countries and cultures. For that reason, managers need to develop tools to enable them to achieve their objectives in a professional manner.

So much for the theory! Many readers will now wonder how this can be implemented especially when they are aware that conflicts can cost a great deal of time and money. This is particularly easy to recognize if you look at soccer teams. These are made up of players from the most diverse cultural backgrounds and a coach – usually for the short time in which they play together – has to form them into a successful team. The fragility and complexity of such teams can be seen from the quick change from success to failure and the regular change of coaches ... and if you do not move with the times, time will see to it that you "move". Coaches who have not mastered the most modern tools are no longer needed. The same applies to players. Therefore, it is possible to draw certain parallels to intercultural project teams. It is important to form the best team and to coach it so that the players in the team can each realize their full potential.

This also applies to executives in an intercultural environment. Project teams or task forces are often put together on an ad hoc basis and have to perform complex tasks in a short time and without the necessary preliminary training. Project managers or team leaders will only achieve the desired results if they succeed in forming the various personalities into an entity that pursues the objectives desired with great commitment.

For this purpose the following requirements need to be met:

- Global managers are always positive. They look at all the diversity and find what can be united and are in a position to build bridges and transform apparent contradictions into synergies.
- They promote the strengths and the well-being of the individual without losing sight of the performance of the entire team.
- They have clear principles that are strong enough to permit exceptions, too.
- They succeed in meeting an internal requirement (for example: the potential of the R & D department) without neglecting the external view (for example: customer wishes and customer requirements).
- They also resolve the apparent contradiction between global integration and local adaptation. Only if they keep on top of things can they find synergistic solutions.
- They are managers who see themselves as servants and not as drivers or controllers. They set framework conditions, within which employees can realize their full potential in the interest of the team, the company, and all stakeholders; and they continue to develop these purposefully. Thus they win the loyalty of both employees and customers.
- They are managers who know the corporate governance models of various national cultures such as the Chinese "Qing-Li-Fa"-Model, in which a relationship (Qing) is established first of all. The quality of the relationship (Li) decides on a collaboration which is implemented in accordance with contractually specified rules (Fa). The relationship is always paramount whereas facts and contracts are more likely to be

given priority in Western leadership styles. They succeed in both: establishing a relationship and achieving clear results.

- Global managers interpret their role as communicator, integrator and project manager on an intercultural basis. They always pursue the objective of combining the strengths of international employees, teams and corporations symbiotically and synergistically in order to improve the learning ability of global organizations, to build up additional competences and to realize above-average profitable growth.

The extent of globalization is still underestimated. Global managers, in particular, who have to travel extensively in their profession like to underestimate the power of national cultures. The values and beliefs expressed therein are not only apparent in the behavior that is visible on the outside. Like the iceberg this only constitutes 10 percent of the specific culture. The remaining 90 percent remains out of sight. As a result, most trade is still conducted within a country or region, such as in a free-trade area like the EU. Despite a growing trend towards internationalization the management of most organizations is still decidedly shaped by the respective local culture and all policies are dominated almost entirely by national interests.

Global managers need to understand cultural differences and actively live this diversity. Consequently, intercultural competence becomes a key qualification for executives and employees of global corporations. Accordingly, an international corporation needs to be in a position to train global specialists and executives.

Global managers need to come to terms with various management cultures. Whereas in industrial countries hierarchies are flattening due to the triumphant advance of knowledge workers, hierarchic and centralistic management structures are still prevalent in countries like China, India and Russia. The choice of location for the holding company is crucial for the development of the corporate culture. As a result, many multi-national corporations relocate various administrative units or even their entire headquarters to growth markets. Apart from the traditional criteria for market attraction, the great appeal of qualified employees and more cultural openness are increasingly taking center stage.

3.6. Intercultural Management and the Role of the Global Manager

The role of a manager is culture-specific whereby the chief concern is decision-making and responsibility. We have learned that a German manager's participative management style tends to be one of delegating responsibility and encouraging employees to act independently and stand on their own two feet. As far as Italian employees are concerned, the manager is the boss. They expect clear guidelines with respect to work content and deadlines. A participative leadership style is more likely to confuse them and they are deceived into doubting the manager's competence.

Intercultural pitfalls do not only arise in the case of obvious and great cultural distance but also within one's own organization with employees who have a different cultural background or come from allegedly similar cultures. In this way, Germany, Austria and Switzerland are three countries that are divided by a common language. Moreover, there are a growing number of employees with a migration background. This means that intercultural competence is required even in everyday situations.

Having successful international executives is a company's major competitive advantage. Developing executives with international knowledge comprises four elements: the four "Ts" – "travel", "teamwork", "training" and "transfers". The influence of executives on the achieving of objectives cannot be overestimated.

Global Managers Today – Requirements and Competences

Due to the challenges in dealing with other cultures and countries, the global managers' role is crucial for the success of any international strategy. They are on the spot and everyday they are confronted with the challenges that a different environment poses. The concept of the "global manager" is to be viewed more as a qualification than a clearly defined hierarchical level or title in a company. Today the title "Head of New Business Development" is frequently used but this can mean many things. Below are the requirements for global managers. It should be stressed that decision-makers in particular should have this qualification and more especially they should have experience locally in order to be capable of making qualified decisions in an international environment. This ought to be taken into consideration when selecting personnel.

The Tasks to be undertaken by Global Managers

Global managers are *good intercultural communicators*. The company is unknown in most of the markets. The managers succeed in obtaining appointments with all the relevant stakeholders and in introducing the company with its positioning, strategy and products and services locally. In the process there will be questions about the objectives in the country in question. The precondition for convincing answers is a clear market strategy.

Global managers are *good integrators* who succeed in building bridges between cultures such as between the individual departments at head-quarters and those in the local subsidiary. They are not only able to find compromises between two different cultures but can create synergies and symbioses, too. As a result, motivated teams are created whose members can jointly overcome the challenges in international management with a strong culture.

Global managers are also *good, experienced project managers*. In this role they are concerned with opening up markets and if necessary with exiting a market. Aware of the challenges, obstacles and problems that cause many foreign projects to fail they are in a position to achieve objectives.

Typical global managers are usually employees in a staff division that reports directly to the management. As head of this division they are responsible for developing country managers, expanding and updating knowledge of foreign markets and supporting the management in implementing their foreign strategy (market entry and exit). In their position they are specialists just like the heads of all the staff divisions.

The Skills required by Global Managers

With regard to *professional competence* and despite specializing in corporate management, global managers are more likely to be *universalists* rather than *specialists* because they often run a subsidiary on their own or in collaboration with local executives. Examples are factory managers who as expatriates only collaborate with local employees, or the heads of branches who ought to have a profound knowledge of finance and law in addition to their own field of sales and services. Moreover, they ought to be familiar with the key corporate functions from their own practical experience and have a feeling for finance and risks.

Social competence rather than professional competence is a more crucial criterion for the selection of global managers. While specialists might be able to compensate their lack of social competence as head of a specialist department, social and especially intercultural competence is indispensable abroad and absolutely crucial for success.

Intercultural competence is based first of all on the global manager's ability to meet foreign cultures with positive curiosity, without prejudice, with respect and great sensitivity. This can only work if it is understood that other cultures are different, neither better nor worse but simply different. It is upon this that *passive cultural adaptation builds*. This also entails accepting behavior that is different, and presupposes a high level of tolerance and discipline to accept somewhat unusual behavior as natural. It also comprises *active cultural adaptation* – i.e. the skill to adapt one's own behavior to the local culture. Obviously it is not a matter of becoming Chinese, Japanese or Russian – in other words adopting the other culture with all its values and beliefs. This would be misunderstood by the majority of local employees and stakeholders. The formerly introverted German engineer would not be taken seriously during his work assignment in Sicily if he were to run through his office gesticulating wildly and talking loudly and were always to arrive too late. Global managers always remain foreigners but they can adapt their behavior without losing their own culture so that communication can be respectful and efficient. This requires taking taboos into account. Global managers always need to know with whom certain matters may be discussed and thus they remain authentic and predictable for local conversation partners. This is best achieved by learning the language of the country in question. Most local conversation partners see this as a positive sign and appreciate it.

Global managers are usually alone when they travel abroad. Like entrepreneurs they have to be able to develop solutions with local employees, decide in favor of one of these and accept responsibility for its consistent implementation. Young companies, in particular, regularly get into tricky situations in an unfamiliar environment. Managers need to keep calm, have to improvise sometimes and need to motivate their employees in difficult situations. The *management competence* needed abroad requires different skills to those in headquarters where diplomatic and political dexterity and the persistent path through committees and hierarchies are more likely to be required. The challenge for global managers lies in the flexible adaptation of their management and communication style to the respective situation.

The last requirement for global managers that should be mentioned here is the ability to establish the corporate strategy worldwide and to preserve the company's reputation even in difficult situations (for example: corruption).

Training Global Managers

Global managers' success is based mainly on the awareness of their specific skills. Like other managers they require appropriate tools and expert knowledge (for example: bookkeeping, human resources, marketing). International management is a separate field of expertise and as such needs to be learned. In international business, global managers are the major growth factor for multi-nationals and for small and medium-sized businesses, too. In addition to developing global managers of one's own, which is a somewhat lengthy process, it is usually advisable to recruit global managers with experience or to purchase expertise from consultants and interim managers.

Tools for Global managers Part 1: Communication Instruments

Your company is unknown abroad. No one knows your name, your product or your brands. Global managers are the company's ambassadors in a new target country and have to inform various (sometimes even critical) stakeholders about their employer and the corporate objectives. Building up trust – it would be even better to develop credibility and predictability – requires detailed and regular communication, according to the motto "Information is Motivation". This requires efficient instruments.

As soon as you ask potential business partners for a meeting, they will not hesitate to look up your company in the Internet. Consequently, it is absolutely essential for you to have a highly informative website which is also in the language of the country in question or at least in the languages that are most common worldwide. It might be appropriate to offer the six official languages of the United Nations: Arabic, Chinese (Mandarin), English, French, Russian and Spanish. Languages that are also common are Hindi/Bengali (in India), Portuguese, German and Japanese. As soon as you are present in a market, a website in the official language of the country is absolutely indispensable. Moreover, the contents should be adapted to the culture of the target country. This applies to such things as content, photos, colors and the use of various media such as films. Detailed information about the company and its products is of advantage to your company in countries with a high propensity to uncertainty avoidance whereas cultures that focus on relationships and are hierarchic appreciate a video message from the CEO.

In the foreign country, global managers will incorporate the advantages of their company's home country into this communication (if this makes sense) in order to position the company and set it apart from competitors. For this purpose he will use the label "Made in …" (for example: Watches – made in Switzerland) to benefit from the image of the particular country. It is important to note the following:

- Intercultural stereotypes with positive connotations can be used to advantage. For example: the discrete Swiss banker; the reliable German engineer, the stylish Italian fashion designer and the French gourmet cook.
- Many countries have a positive image with regards to certain products. For example: Japan for consumer electronics, the USA for high technology or Russia and Australia for raw materials.
- The image of the country also impinges on the price-quality ration. For example: German products are of very high quality, Japanese are innovative and Chinese are the cost leader.

Global managers will not communicate contents that tend to be national in character. Sponsoring the sports club in one's home town or a huge local event will meet with little interest in another country. Unfortunately this still meets with a lack of understanding in ethnocentric headquarters.

Due to spatial and cultural distance it is important to have a manual and a brochure in the foreign country on the vision, the values, the culture, the strategy and the objectives of the company. This also applies to company and product brochures that ought to have a clear description of the product and all the services provided.

Ultimately global managers are ambassadors whose tasks include establishing and cultivating a network in the country in question. Suitable tools are for example events with the local Chamber of Commerce, an export promotion agency or an ambassador/consulate.

Tools for Global Managers Part 2: Leadership Instruments

Every initial situation requires its own management instruments. On account of the great distance from headquarters, the different culture, the different environment, the unknown quality of the brand and other differences, too, global managers implement new management instruments and adapt those already in existence according to their own requirements. The following examples show how global managers can improve their efficiency perceptibly by selecting the right management instruments. In many cases clear guidelines are more likely to be of help. As a rule it is advisable to delegate decision-making to the respective local companies as far as possible.

Information Material for Companies

The huge distance from headquarters makes it difficult for employees and other stakeholders to really identify with the parent company (for example with its culture). For that reason global managers need instruments to help them transfer the vision, the culture and the values of the company (for example with regard to time orientation/punctuality, responsibility, reliability or quality of work) and instruct and train local employees accordingly. The objective is efficient communication at the interfaces between the local company and its parent and affiliated companies.

Thus it happens that documents – such as company brochures containing the visions, values and objectives of the company – that are frequently regarded as superfluous at headquarters are only fully effective abroad. Employees and other stakeholders make use of this instrument to identify with the company and to provide information for their environment. (Question: Where do you work?). This also applies to the annual report. It is imperative that both documents are available in the local language and are supplemented with other media (for example: a company video).

Internal Directives and Guidelines

Internal management manuals or standards, such as project management, data security, maintenance and cleanliness of company property or reporting, help global managers to convey the organizational culture and its practices. They give precise details on the behavior that is expected with respect to time and quality and are thus an important reference point for employees

Motivation and Incentive Schemes

It is crucial that guidelines and instruments provide global managers with flexibility and scope. This is of paramount importance for motivation and incentive schemes. The differences are comparable with the difference between the cultures. Therefore effective remuneration and incentive schemes need to take the cultural differences and customs in the respective countries and branches into consideration. At all events, a globally comparable remuneration scheme (frequently with management shares) that reflects the organizational culture can be developed for the country managers/managing directors of the individual local companies. At other / lower local management levels it is essential to use local remuneration schemes.

Tools for Global managers Part 3:
Mediation Process for Bridging Cultural Distances

Dealing with cultural differences between countries is still neglected in most companies. Despite a keen awareness of the problem, the necessary measures in the form of training and mediation processes are not always implemented efficiently even though intercultural collaboration, especially in international project teams, is crucial for success.

The basic idea of the mediation process (see Fig. 36) is creating the synergistic balance between local responsiveness and the desire for global integration with a view to implementing the business plan for the target market jointly and successfully. An initial step requires all the employees in the project to become aware of their own culture, to communicate their responsiveness and to recognize the differences from the cultures of their colleagues. Cultural profiles are used for this purpose. The prerequisite is that there is a clear and open acknowledgement of the existence of cultural differences.

A second step entails working out both cultural differences and commonalities. The latter provide the foundation for collaboration whereas the cultural differences provide the basis for the search for synergies and

Fig. 36: Mediation process for bridging cultural differences

symbioses. It is important to note that simple compromises reduce the effectiveness of an intercultural team and make further conflicts and poor results inevitable.

Executives and employees should be trained in intercultural competence which should be brushed up continually. Usually this can be done in seminars and workshops. Building up intercultural competence is also one of the tasks of the market development process *"company2newmarket"*. In Step 2 "Market Preparation", the topic of cultural differences is addressed directly and trained constantly from the moment the international project team begins work.

Tools for Global managers Part 4:
Behavior in Critical Situations

Today, one of the major values a company has is its reputation. It takes a long time to build up a reputation but only a few seconds to destroy it which usually results in considerable economic costs. Therefore, the aim in difficult situations is primarily to preserve the reputation of the company even if this might mean economic disadvantages initially.

Companies abroad are under continuous observation. This applies both to large corporations and to small and medium sized businesses. The company's activities abroad are not only observed by supervisory bodies, NGOs and other stakeholders (for example: unions) in the home country but are also observed by the same or similar stakeholders in the host country. The view abroad is usually more critical because a reputation still has to be established there.

Most companies are aware of this fact and try to build up a good reputation with a communications department at the highest level in the hierarchy, detailed codes of conduct for all employees and the use of all kinds of certification and seals of quality (for example: best employer, Fair Trade, global reporting). This centralized approach soon reaches its limits abroad and actually always has a negative impact. Nothing else can be expected in view of the long reaction times, the poor quality of translations, answers that are not adapted to the culture and written by someone anonymous (for example: press releases). Consequently, it is crucial that global managers are in a position to and are empowered to deal with difficult situations.

Global managers can get into difficulty very quickly in a foreign country. They have to take a decision that (at best) complies with the law of the host country but not the law or the morals of their home country or the location of headquarters. In this dilemma, that cannot always be assigned to clear rules, it is useful to have a preliminary decision tree, for example. This outlines the process of applying various aids to decision-making (see Fig. 37). First of all global managers should ask whether taking this decision will mean that they will be breaking the law of their home country, of the location of headquarters or the host country. Next they should take general principles, internal corporate values and the opinions of their immediate superiors into account. Involving the latter is important even though these may not always have a detailed knowledge of the market. Finally global managers ought to consult their own values and beliefs and their conscience, too. In practice it is very helpful to rely on philosophical and religious values that are common to both cultures.

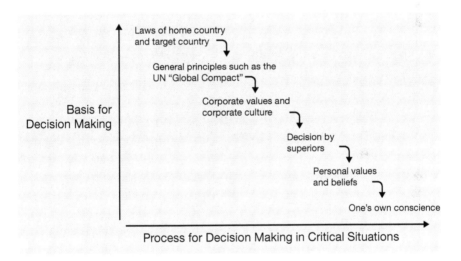

Fig. 37: Model of a decision tree in critical situations

An example of general principles (the second step of the decision tree) is the UN Global Compact. It describes ten principles on human rights, labor, environment and anti-corruption. Of course, these principles are open to a wide range of interpretation that in turn depends on the culture. Nevertheless, they are very suitable as a basis for even more specifically formulated corporate values and behavior patterns (the third step of the decision tree). This example shows that the individual steps of the decision tree build on each other and therefore ought to be processed one after the other.

1. Principle	Compliance with international human rights
2. Principle	No complicity in human rights abuse
3. Principle	Upholding the freedom of association and recognizing employees' rights to collective bargaining
4. Principle	Compliance with the elimination of forced labor
5. Principle	Compliance with the abolition of child labor
6. Principle	Compliance with the elimination of discrimination in respect of employment and occupation
7. Principle	Precautionary approach to environmental challenges
8. Principle	Promotion of environmental responsibility
9. Principle	Development and diffusion of environmentally friendly technologies
10. Principle	Work against corruption in all forms including extortion and bribery

Table 14: UN Global Compact

It is impossible to entirely avoid errors especially in an international environment. The most credible approach is well-considered, prompt and transparent communication in conjunction with speedy implementation. This means correcting the error and making a generous claims settlement followed by considerable investments in marketing.

Tools for Global Managers Part 5:
Overseas Assignment Cycle for Expatriates

People make the difference here. Employees in another country are ambassadors of a company, its culture and its values. At the same time it is irrelevant whether the employee is an expatriate (on overseas assignment from group headquarters), an inpatriate (on overseas assignment from a foreign branch) or a transpatriate (on overseas assignment from one foreign company to a different foreign company). In point of fact what is crucial is the ability of those in the project team to adapt and transfer their knowledge and experiences to other foreign markets.

In practice, the overseas assignment cycle in four steps has proved practical (see Fig. 38). The main criterion for selection is the ability of expatriates and their families, as the case may be, to integrate into the new culture and to meet the demands of the job there. As they act as representatives of the company, criteria such as manners and values acquire considerable significance. In the second step the expatriates and their families are prepared for the actual overseas assignment. During the overseas assignment it is crucial that they never lose touch with the parent company. To this end each of them is given a mentor in the upper management. The last step of a successful overseas assignment is their return. Frequently the mistake is made that the former expatriate is not offered an adequate job or the family is not given support in coping with re-integration problems. For that reason many expatriates turn their backs on the company within a short space of time.

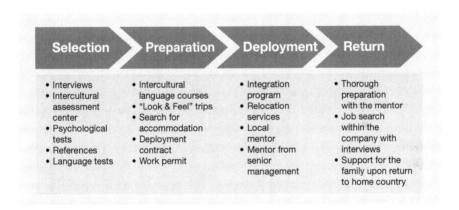

Fig. 38: Overseas assignment cycle in four steps for expatriates

Integration into a new culture takes place in four steps (see Fig. 38). At the beginning the enthusiasm for the new country and the new culture is great. In this phase the differences from the home land are interpreted positively. After the first negative experiences which inevitably arise in a different culture the depression phase sets in. Unlike the first phase, the new environment in particular is seen in a negative light. After the next phases of "initial adaptation" and "disillusionment" the new culture and the new country are accepted in the fifth phase and the expatriate has succeeded in adapting.

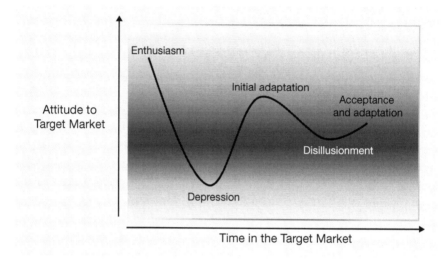

Fig. 39: Intercultural integration process of expatriates at the place of overseas assignment

In this process advice and close support by the project team and the international HR department are important. The majority of expatriates abandon their overseas assignment during the phases "disillusionment" and "depression". The usual reason is the family. Unlike expatriates who meet up with (relatively) familiar structures at their workplace, the families are completely immersed into the culture. Usually everything in another culture is different, whether it is shopping, school, trades people, doctors or friends. On account of the high risk, therefore, it is advisable to have professional support.

Integration into local networks is aimed at meeting important opinion-leaders and decision-makers in this market. This way, companies are informed in good time about new trends and have time to react appropriately. In a second step one's own points of view can be incorporated into the network and might even influence the formation of opinions on major topics.

Tools for building up a local network are for example participation in selected events, arranging so-called "lunch-meetings" and cultivating contacts in a data bank. Later this is supplemented by active PR policies, appearances as a guest speaker or involvement in associations. Today, social networks are a significant factor on account of their global focus. Recommendations through personal contacts facilitate integration into local society perceptibly. In many countries the services of specialized PR agencies can also be used.

Usually, personal experience and knowledge count for practically nothing in foreign markets. Frequently, global managers are unaware of this fact. They require instruments to help them to communicate better and to reach better decisions in the foreign country. The tools presented here deliberately concentrate on collaboration with people. In my experience it is the quality of the relationship to employees and external stakeholders in the foreign market that is the key success factor apart from good management that is appropriate to the specific culture.

Summary

International management is always intercultural management. Diversity does not only provide global companies with enormous opportunities but is simply indispensible. However it involves appreciable risks. Global managers and the entire organization need to face this challenge successfully and develop diversity and intercultural management into one of their competitive advantages.

At the same time what always counts is the efficiency of organizations and their ability to learn in order to build up new competences, to obtain the best qualified employees and to realize an above-average profitable growth. In a global environment this can only be achieved by increasing intercultural competence at all company levels. The tools presented here are easy to learn, can be adapted quickly to the specific requirements of a company and can be integrated into intercultural workshops and seminars without any problems.

In this process it is important for employees to learn about their own culture first. Only then will they be in a position to adapt their behavior to the corporate culture and aspire to successful collaboration with colleagues from other cultures. However, in this case it is not a question of looking for simple compromises. Collaboration in international and intercultural teams only works if synergies and symbioses develop that make use of the strengths of every individual. This objective places enormous demands on executives who have to build bridges to unite apparent contradictions.

In the case of a crisis with severe interpersonal conflicts or problems in a foreign market, global managers react according to their own culture. Thus, a global manager from a country with high uncertainty avoidance might increase controls, visit the subsidiary frequently and implement even more rules and processes regardless of the culture of the country in question or irrespective of whether strengthening the relationship to the local stakeholder might be more successful. The real test for assessing the success of intercultural training and instruments is a crisis.

Lessons to be learned

1. *The key to any culture is its language:* It is advisable to gain at least some basic knowledge of the national language, to spend some time in the country and to participate in the life of the local population.
2. *Other cultures are different, neither better nor worse, but simply different:* Cultural differences exist. There is no denying the fact. It is a question of understanding them and not evaluating them. The prerequisite for understanding cultural differences is knowledge of one's own culture.
3. *Bear the "self-reference criterion" in mind:* People evaluate every communication from the perspective of their own culture. This leads inevitably to misunderstandings. In crisis situations people always fall back on well-tried behavior patterns and the experiences they have had in their own cultures. In cases of doubt these are always useless in other cultures. Regrettably this is never known until afterwards.
4. *Cultural synergies and symbioses instead of simple compromises:* Multi-cultural organizations cannot be managed on the basis of simple compromises but only by uniting the strengths of diverse cultures symbiotically and synergistically.

5. *Cultural profiles cannot be transferred to individuals*: Cultural profiles always portray the culture of a people in its entirety and from the mean value of all the test candidates. Never succumb to the danger of generalizing but treat every human being as a unique individual.
6. *Cultural profiles as tools for intercultural communication*: Cultural profiles help all employees to operate successfully in an intercultural environment. Ensuring efficient communication increases the quality of collaboration in international teams.
7. *Diversity as the basis for competitive advantage*: Diversity in international companies is not only a factor for success but in the meantime has become a prerequisite for success.
8. *Combining contradictions such as global integration and local adaptation*: A global manager can dissolve apparent contradictions and build bridges.
9. *Corporate culture as a melting pot*: The corporate culture is a professional "melting pot" for diverse national cultures.
10. *Behavior in critical situations*: The reputation of the company is gaining ever increasing significance. Consequently global managers and expatriates need clear guidelines as to how to behave in difficult situations.
11. *Attention to reintegration shocks in the overseas assignment cycle of expatriates*: Without adequate preparation there are adaptation shocks with every change of abode, whether upon arrival abroad or upon return to the home country.

Conclusion: Success Factors for Global Organizations

Today, an increasing number of organizations, ranging from private or non-profit making to government organizations, have to establish themselves in an international environment. There are many examples of successful internationalization. A vast number of organizations of varying

Fig. 40: Global Management Model

size, with various resources and business models from cultural institutes like the Goethe Institute or China's Confucius Institute, non-profit-making organizations like Transparency International, SOS Children's Villages or the WWF and sports associations (FIFA, IOC) to the many private SMEs in German-speaking countries operate very successfully all over the globe. Nevertheless, the majority of all internationalization projects come to grief. The causes are seldom mentioned. They vanish more or less without trace. Only the success stories are reported at great length.

Regardless of their business model, successful international organizations have a great deal in common. The major success factors are part of my Global Management Model. Among other things, tools based on the results of an international strategy assessment are used to develop international strategies, to enter markets; to deal with other cultures and to gain and process information on foreign markets (cf. Fig. 40). Their successful implementation is checked continually. Below is a brief outline of my own success factors and tips for employees with contacts abroad.

1. Development of a Truly Global Vision and a Competitive International Strategy

Globally successful organizations have an international perspective. They see themselves as global market leaders in their market niche. These niches are often very small so that it is only with the global marketing of their product that they achieve the quantities necessary to finance development costs and to reach more competitive production costs.

Concentrating on a market niche or product affords the company a clear positioning which is constantly expanded by additional (application) innovations and services. However, the role of market leader does not only mean economic advantages. It also has great psychological significance. Customers, employees and other stakeholders, too, prefer to collaborate with the market leader. This opens doors, increases identification and helps establish a strong brand.

Companies that have an international strategy provide themselves with an organization with which they succeed in achieving their global objectives. Classic one-product companies prefer a functional organization whereas diversified enterprises are more likely to use a transnational organization structure. Moreover, they concentrate on building up core competences and competitive advantages which are also relevant to their international clients and customers and can be transferred to other foreign markets and cultures.

SMEs from German-speaking countries are an example of successful internationalization. These companies are often owned and run by families and stand out due to their long-term perspective and their high share of equity. Consequently, they do not break off their market entry as soon as they experience the first setbacks and are more likely to withstand the pressure to reach short-term compromises. As a result they are able to establish a strong position in their target markets in the long term. Good illustrations of this are German family-owned companies like Knauf, Faber-Castell, Giesecke & Devrient or Rittal.

2. Using a Structured Market Entry and Development Process

Developing new foreign markets still presents most organizations with a huge challenge. They are torn between the high costs and risks of developing an international market and the chance of profitable growth. Usually, questions like "Will the products catch on?", "Can our price expectations be put across?" or "Which sales volume is achievable?" can only really be answered after market entry has taken place.

It is not only a matter of inexperience. Quite often the requisite knowledge is missing and there is a lack of important contacts locally. Therefore, the choice of foreign markets is likely to depend on subjective criteria such as the current press or the circle of friends in the country club instead of objective criteria that are imposed by a structured market entry process. Well-known negative spin-offs are precipitous market exits and a spate of business trips which have no positive economic impact. In this case market entry for these organizations is usually little more than an incalculable adventure with repercussions that frequently threaten their very existence.

Standardized processes like the market entry process *company2new-market* enable an organization to build up new foreign markets with fewer resources and fewer risks and to achieve sustainable growth there.

Therefore, internationalization becomes a core competence or even a major competitive advantage. Only the organization that manages to be one of the first to place their products and services globally will become a market leader.

3. Train your Employees to Develop Outstanding Intercultural Competence

Globally successful companies manage to obtain the best employees independent of their origins or culture. In this geocentric selection of personnel it is not only the professional criteria that count. Fitting in with the corporate culture is paramount. At the same time companies act like professional sports teams. Employees have to integrate into the team with their personality and skills and help to make it even more successful.

In this respect the HR department is a kind of gate-keeper. The international growth of the company and the implementation of the processes of change always depend on the right employees. It is the HR department's responsibility to find the right employees and integrate and develop these. Developing their intercultural competence is particularly crucial. The objective is the efficient integration of employees independent of their culture. In the process, they learn the values of the organizational culture, and its symbols and rituals. This entails also collaboration in intercultural teams and with external stakeholders such as customers and suppliers. The objective is always a symbiotic and synergetic collaboration that makes efficient use of the strengths of the specific cultures.

Global SMEs in particular are very successful in this respect. They have a corporate organizational culture, have deep local roots but are also sensitive to cultures and have a cosmopolitan outlook; they are very performance oriented but intolerant of employees whose performance is below par. They succeed in obtaining qualified employees and retaining them over the long term because due to their global positioning and a high share in the net value added they offer interesting and responsible positions with fast decision-making channels. In addition they seldom suffer from being grossly overstaffed. To be sure, this has one disadvantage – human resources can be scarce – but it increases efficiency significantly.

By establishing intercultural competence an international organization is more quickly in a position to obtain, integrate and retain better qualified employees from other cultures. Collaboration between international project teams and organizational units with various functions and from different countries becomes more efficient. Just like all the members of a sports team, all the players – independent of their origin – contribute to the entire team with their individual strengths.

4. Manage your Global Value Chain Professionally

The majority of successful international organizations control their value chain themselves. This starts with securing access to raw materials. Frequently, production takes place with machines and tools they have developed themselves. In selecting a market entry form they dispense with partnerships; similarly they do without outsourcing for manufacturing and services. Communication is centered on customer requirements and solutions. Thus complexity is reduced, controllability is simplified, proximity to the customer is maintained and knowledge remains in the company. Consequently, competitors are scarcely in a position to copy the business model and intellectual property.

The majority of successful international organizations have global value chains. Whereas NPOs' customers are donators in developed markets, they receive assistance in less developed foreign markets. MNEs produce or buy in foreign markets with cost savings and sell their products mainly in foreign markets where they can achieve attractive profit margins. Even the activities and the target groups vary in the different foreign markets between fund raising and implementing aid projects – i.e. purchasing/production and selling. All these activities have to be integrated globally into a value chain.

Building up and using knowledge about foreign markets and one's own value chain is therefore a core task of the global manager. The International Market Monitor is a Business Intelligence Software that helps global managers to recognize opportunities and challenges more swiftly than their competitors abroad and to take better decisions.

5. Consistent Use of Global Advantages

Champions in internationalization are rigorous in exploiting global advantages. They analyze foreign markets continually in order to recognize the opportunities and risks more quickly than their competitors. They adapt their products to other cultures and local requirements without dispensing with the advantages of global platforms for brands, intellectual property, production and technology as well as the differences in costs and regulations in the various foreign markets.

International market leaders succeed in improving their cost position on the one hand and the quality of their product portfolio on the other hand. In this way they set the standard for their products and technology in their market niche, are able to achieve higher prices and build up customer loyalty which is achieved mainly by manufacturing entire components, by the high quality of the product, reliability (e.g. reliable deliveries, minimum downtimes) and cost effectiveness or a lower total cost of ownership.

Thus they avoid the error made by many organizations that forgo attractive contribution margins in the present because of the prospect of future economies of scale due to an increase in sales abroad. Coordination and project costs very quickly devour low margins especially in small subsidiaries. In that case, the global manager has to react immediately and naturally this succeeds better with forms of market entry and market growth that are subject to his complete control (for example: export, subsidiary).

6. Dealing Actively with Crises

Today sustainability is a major success factor and a good reputation is the prerequisite for the economic success of a company. Frequently, changes in management and economic crises, too, have a radical impact on internationalization strategies that have been successful up to that point. After internationalization activities have been stopped, it often happens that only "internationalization ruins" remain despite a series of restructuring and cost cutting measures. As there are no clear growth strategies, positioning and competitive advantages, they are rarely profitable and wander like "zombies" in their particular foreign markets. Thus the home market which is usually very profitable finances an expensive foreign investment and holding structures until the management finally attempts to solve the problem.

In this respect family-owned companies and enterprises from cultures with high long-term orientation are at an advantage. They have a long-term perspective which they pursue with great discipline and rapid decision-making channels, and usually with the right employees, too. This means among other things overcoming crises and, after notching up the first successes, continuing to invest in the foreign market to achieve the market objectives desired. They have come to stay. Forgoing "hit-and-run" strategies also creates trust and predictability, the two cornerstones for a good reputation.

After crises and even after the first successes on the market, many companies cease to invest any further in their foreign subsidiary. They attempt to achieve their objectives solely with internal growth. This is difficult to understand because a subsidiary that is too small can only participate in market growth to a limited extent and the profits will be devoured to a large extent by the co-ordination costs.

Nowadays, all organizations need to position themselves globally. Gone are the days when political risks could at least be ignored in industrial countries. Today, an increase in state bureaucratization, a rise in taxes and duties and the simultaneous restriction of rights and security – whether legal security, public safety or the protection of property – dominate. Organizations of any kind can only avoid these increasingly poorer framework conditions by spreading the risks over several foreign markets.

Dealing with crises and implementing market exits are thus part of the global managers' day to day operations. They are aware that the profitability of their international organizations depends initially on the profits but also substantially on avoiding the unexpectedly high cost of market entry, market exit and depreciations of production losses or claims on insolvent customers.

7. Attitudes

The success of global managers also depends on their attitudes. They stand out on account of their *respect and humility* in the face of their task and especially in the face of other cultures. They succeed in resolving the apparent extremes between cultures or, for example, between local adaption and global standardization and adopt a positive attitude in striving for solutions even in the most difficult situations.

Global managers know themselves. They understand that in cases of doubt their own knowledge and experiences in a foreign market do not count. Nevertheless, they are always prepared to *learn* and possess the ability to make use of efficient tools to find a successful solution to the most complex tasks.

Global managers do not allow themselves to be guided by prejudice and stereotypes in the context of intercultural collaboration. They are curious and open when looking for the strengths of other cultures and integrate these into their organizations very successfully. They work effectively with employees, colleagues, and executives from other cultures but do not forget where they come from.

Like diplomats, global managers are intermediaries between the needs of the local subsidiaries and corporate headquarters. In most companies their greatest challenge is not the developing of new foreign markets but dealing with internal doubters. *Applying the* Global Management Model *provides global managers with a tool to create mainly stable framework conditions within a company for a professional and successful international market development and to expand this to a permanent and sustainable competitive advantage.*

Appendix: From Local EU Sales Markets to Global Growth Markets

The flagship of the German economy – the automotive industry – is an impressive example of how companies which are strongly positioned on *global growth markets* achieve record turnover and an increase in profit whereas companies whose focus is on the near-by sales markets of the EU are subject to sustainable, economic challenges.

Globalisation is necessary

Thus, Europe's national debt crisis is having a boomerang effect especially on EU-SMEs that principally export to the EU. Only a consistent reorientation of international strategy can put companies back on track. What is decisive in this case is a professional implementation with tried and tested methods in order to gain new long-term customers in new international markets – with justifiable risks and the controlled deployment of financial and human resources.

Most EU-SMEs expand in countries which are member states of the EU. Thanks to exports, licensing or their own sales representatives a huge, mainly homogeneous economic and currency area opened up which only required manageable effort and expense. Apart from cultural and linguistic obstacles the individual risks of each country played only a secondary role especially for (indirect) exporters.

The national debt crisis has meant that the *country risk* is increasingly becoming the focus of attention again. A decline in sales figures, an increase in fiscal pressure and pressure on margins as well as write-offs of receivables from state and private debtors are reducing the attraction of markets not only of the GIPS in Southern Europe for some time to come. Consequently, rapidly increasing *corruption* in Greece has meanwhile reached the same level as in Columbia and Djibouti. The development of GDP is heading exactly in this negative direction, too. Therefore, SMEs will have to act quickly if they wish to avoid a further loss in revenue and assets.

Globalisation which has now become necessary instead of *regionalisation* or the focussing on global growth markets instead of local EU sales markets demands a perceptible *professionalization of international management*. It is only with tools that have been tried and tested and are easy to use that international managers can successfully cope with the increasing complexity.

International Market Development

The *management process "company2newmarket"* is an example of the increasing *professionalization of international management*. By applying this process, *companies find new customers on new international markets in less time; at the same time they require fewer resources and face fewer risks*. The process is composed of four logical steps; each consists of a large number of tasks which are carried out using standardised tools. It is not until one step has been completed and the respective milestone and objectives have been attained that the international manager can begin the next step whereby the management and the opening up of a multitude of various markets is less difficult because the different projects are more easily compared, are more efficient and more transparent, and complexity is reduced.

Step 1: Market evaluation and selection

The objective of Step 1 is the *evaluation and selection of attractive markets overseas* for one's own company. Based on one's own competitive strengths, competences, resources and competitive advantages, the market of each country is examined by means of a filter consisting of three steps and with company–specific criteria, and results in a list of countries with the most attractive target markets.

Step 2: Market preparation

The objective of Step 2 is *preparing for entry of the target markets* selected in Step 1 whereby answers are found to operative questions, for example, about locations, employees, products, processes and the foundation of the company in question, and this leads to a comprehensive and workable business and financial plan.

Step 3: Market entry

The objective of Step 3 is the practical *implementation of the business model on the new international market* and the evidence of the efficiency and profitability of the core processes or rather the carrying through of the exporter's own price expectations. In this respect, the international customers you have and whom you already serve on the respective local market and those of your employees who have a cultural link with the target country can frequently be helpful.

Step 4: Market development and growth

The objective of Step 4 is *growth* with a view to achieving both the desired market position and the planned sales and profit targets. For this purpose every internal and external market growth form is available. This also comprises setting up local organisation structures, localising management and integrating all of these into the management and communication structures of the entire company.

Strategic reorientation

The *reorientation of international strategy* is based on three mainstays. First of all, the current situation of the international businesses is analysed and assessed. From this a market-specific approach is derived and implemented professionally with scientifically and practically tested instruments such as the management process – *"company2newmarket"* – as described above.

Securing of assets

In the markets of countries with a sharp and fast decline in market attractiveness (e.g. GIPS and some of MENA) the *securing of assets* is paramount. One alternative is the *sale of the subsidiary* – with or without a call-option – to the local management (= MBO). In this way access to the market remains secure, risks are reduced and resources are available for the growth markets. Further solutions are the transfer of local stocks and accounts (= cash pooling) or the reduction of costs by centralising and by implementing innovative technologies.

Investing in growth markets

The resources which become available are invested in the *opening of new global growth markets*. This differs subject to the sector and the business model. The markets of Brazil, Russia, India, China, South Korea, Indonesia, Mexico and Turkey, which each have a share of at least one per cent of the global GNP, are incorporated under the label "Growth8" and might be among the most attractive.

Market entry is to take place step by step starting with low-risk *market entry forms* such as *exports* and *contract manufacturing*, and culminating in the founding of the *company's own sales organisation and factories*. In the market entry phase co-operation with specialist consultants and government foreign trade organisations such as the Swiss Office for Promoting Foreign Trade and Commerce or the German Chambers of Commerce Abroad is recommended.

Making use of Technologies

Modern communication and information technologies are a crucial driver for access to global growth markets. A comprehensive website suffices to provide the basic information required by all interested stakeholder groups world-wide. A supplementary *online shop* can furnish customers globally with information on products and services and their specifications and link them with the respective contact partners via social media. However it is important to integrate the individual communication instruments so that the international manager receives the best possible support because in most cultures face-to-face contact is still the most decisive aspect.

Securing IP rights

The *securing of one's own IP rights* and their incorporation in a company in a suitable location opens additional revenue potential by licensing to one's own and other companies and affords protection – at least to some degree – against uncontrolled reproductions. In addition, the active management of liability risks is decisive for the survival of a company. Should it not be possible to avoid this with suitable measures such as insurance cover, it should, at least, never endanger the core of the company.

Conclusion

The future of a company and competition are no longer decided in Europe but elsewhere. There is a shift in global economic balance – and this has been recognized by every company in the meantime. Persevering on the home market is not an alternative. Clear decisions as well as consistent and professional action are required on the way to global growth markets i.e. to the adaptation to new realities. Many SMEs are the "hidden champions" who have become global market leaders in their niche because they have succeeded in opening new international markets more rapidly and more efficiently than their competitors. *Thus, international market development has become a core competence and a sustainable competitive advantage.* There are more than enough examples of such success. Now, the challenge is to transfer these experiences to your own company in order to emerge as one of the victors in this new globalisation.

Glossary

A

Adaptation: This is one of the elements of the 4A-Strategy. It means that products, marketing, and processes need to be adapted as far as possible to local clients' needs as well as to the social, economic, and climatic conditions in a specific foreign market.

Aggregation: This is one of the elements of the 4A-Strategy. It means that a company should use global product, production, brand / marketing and service platforms to benefit from global cost advantages.

Analysis: This is one of the elements of the 4A-Strategy. It means that a company must permanently screen the developments in foreign markets to benefit from market opportunities and to react to negative changes in market attractiveness.

Arbitrage: Arbitrage is one of the elements of the 4A-Strategy. It means that a company should use the advantages in each foreign market such as knowledge, regulation, taxes or HR costs.

B

Blue ocean strategy: This strategy suggests that every organisation should create new demand in new international markets rather than compete directly with its competitors.

Born (again) global: These are companies that, due to their global business model, internationalize early in their existence.

BRIC: Abbreviation for a group of countries – in this case Brazil, Russia, India, and China – with similar characteristics.

C

CAGE differences: The CAGE differences define the cultural, administrative, geographic, and economic differences between two countries.

Centralization: In centralized organisations decision-making takes place at global headquarters.

Chaebol: This is the South-Korean word for conglomerate. A single owner controls a large part of the value chain through one or several loosely connected companies (networks).

Company2newmarket: This is the name of a management process for entering new international markets. It helps companies to develop their international management expertise.

Competitive advantage of nations: Historically or geographically countries have certain competences. These can be core competences or even become a competitive advantage if clients regard it as relevant, sustainable, difficult to copy, and better than all its competitors.

Convergence of management tools: The MNE should use identical or at least similar management styles and tools in all its local market companies to manage them and to create a global corporate culture.

Consistency: The level of consistency in an MNE describes the analogousness of activities in all its global subsidiaries. Consistency in output such as consistent product quality and service delivery can be distinguished from consistency in behaviour such as consistency in how we interact and communicate.

Cultural distance: The distance between two cultures or countries is calculated according to the results of the Hofstede analysis. It is based on the assumption that a high cultural distance generally increases the market entry risk and leads to the selection of a low risk market entry form.

Cultural profile: A cultural profile consists of the differences and specifics in behaviour between two different cultures or countries.

D

Decentralization: Decentralization takes place when a company grants its subsidiaries abroad a high degree of autonomy. In a coordinated decentralization, headquarters provide the corporate strategy and local subsidiaries are free to implement it in their market under the control of and in consultation with headquarters.

Diversity: Diversity describes the differences between countries and cultures. MNEs try to benefit from these differences in numbers (for example: diverse structure of the workforce to access certain markets) and behaviour (for example: knowledge exchange) to gain a competitive advantage.

DTA double taxation agreement: DTAs are bilateral agreements to regulate cross-border taxation between two countries.

E

Efficiency seekers: Companies that attempt to get the most economic production resources (including raw materials in international markets).

EMEA: Abbreviation for a group of countries and regions – in this case Europe, Middle East, and Africa – with similar characteristics.

Emerging markets: An emerging market is a market where part of the infrastructure provided by developed markets is missing.

Ethnocentrism: Description of an international company with a strong focus on the home country and a preference for personnel from the home country and from the home culture for managing and operating the local market companies.

Expatriate: An employee who is sent from headquarters to a local market for a limited time. Inpatriates are employees from international markets who start working at the headquarters of a company. Transpatriates are employees working in the subsidiary in one market and are sent to another international market.

Expansion platform / hub: This is an organisational design element which is located in an attractive region like Dubai, Singapore, or Luxembourg for example and from where the market entry into all regional country markets is coordinated.

Expatriate foreign deployment process: This management process consists of the four steps selection, preparation, deployment, and repatriation.

F

First mover: The first mover strategy is a market timing strategy. The first mover is a company which is the first to enter a foreign market.

Follower strategies: The follower strategy is a market timing strategy. A follower follows the first mover into a market. Early followers who enter relatively fast behind the first movers can be distinguished from late followers.

Forum shopping: Forum shopping defines a strategy by companies to look for the best suitable jurisdiction or location to do business.

Free trade agreement: Two nations sign a free trade agreement to facilitate trade. If more than two nations sign this FTA, they form what is known as a free trade area.

Free trade area: This is the least restrictive and loosest form of economic integration among countries. In these designated areas, goods are traded without monetary and non-monetary trade barriers (e.g. duties, technical standards).

G

Geocentrism: This word describes an international company with a global orientation and a preference for choosing personnel, systems, and ways of managing and operating based on qualifications rather than on nationality or culture.

Global corporate culture: Each MNE should create its own culture, which is to be identical in all local market companies. Tools for communicating the culture are management tools and styles, company visions and values, and marketing material like websites.

Global efficiency versus local responsiveness: The dilemma of international organization theory between local market requirements and the potential of global synergies. The solution is often called "Think global – act local".

Global Manager: The concept of the "global manager" is to be viewed more as a qualification to manage international organizations than a clearly defined hierarchical level or title in a company.

Good corporate citizen: This is a company which is fully integrated into a local market and which is recognized by all its stakeholders as a valuable part of society.

Growth8: This is a group of eight fast growing emerging markets (Brazil, Russia, India, China, Mexico, South-Korea, Turkey and Indonesia) whose national GDP is at least one per cent of the Global GDP.

H

Handover: This word defines the final task in step 4 of the management process *company2newmarket*. The new market company is finally integrated into the organization structure of the MNE and looses its status as a project.

Hidden champion: This is generally an SME which is a global market leader in its market niche.

I

Industrial cluster: This is a loosely connected group of companies (e.g. suppliers, producers, sales channels, service providers etc.) of one industry in a foreign country or region which might internationalize together.

International codes of conduct: The codes of conduct of four major international institutions provide guidelines for MNEs.

International market development: The development of new international markets describe the evaluation, selection, preparation, entry, and the development of new international markets as described in the management process *company2newmarket*.

K

Keiretsu: This is a group of companies (industrial cluster, conglomerate) in Japan with interlocking shareholdings and business relationships.

Key-Driver-Analysis: Key drivers are the characteristics of a product or a service which motivate a potential customer to buy the product or to use the service. A key-driver analysis also includes the sectors value added, low yield, and entry tickets.

Knowledge-to-assumption ratio: This ratio defines the relationship between assumptions and knowledge about a local market. During the management process *company2newmarket* assumptions should be replaced by knowledge. It helps to understand how fast an organization is able to learn.

L

Localization of management: This is part of the handover criteria. A local management is trained and deployed to reduce the number of expatriates.

M

Market attractiveness portfolio: This portfolio shows the markets analyzed according to their attractiveness and based on the two criteria "market attractiveness" and "internal strength". It is used to summarize the results of step 1 and as a tool to select a market entry form.

Market concentration strategy: This is a market expansion policy which is characterized by a sequential market entry (one market after another).

Market entry: This is the third step of the management process *company2newmarket*. The objective of this step is to launch the new market company successfully using the business model defined in step two.

Market entry barriers: Barriers to prevent a market entry.

Market entry forms: Companies can choose between different forms when they wish to enter a market. At first, they have to decide whether they want to buy a local market company or to build it up. If they have decided to build it up, they can again choose between different market entry forms such as export, franchising, or the foundation of a subsidiary.

Market entry motives: Companies generally go to new markets because they are seeking new sales markets, higher efficiency of resources, new resources or strategic assets.

Market entry strategy: Companies can choose an active or passive market entry strategy. The approach used in active market entry strategies can be experienced-based, option-based, and market-research based.

Market evaluation and selection: This is the first step of the management process *company2newmarket*. The objective of this step is to evaluate new international markets and to select the most attractive markets to enter.

Market exit barriers: Barriers to prevent a market exit.

Market development and growth: This is the fourth and final step of the management process *company2newmarket*. The goal of this step is to rollout the complete business model, to integrate the new market company into the local market, and to achieve the handover criteria.

Market growth forms: These are generally identical with market entry forms but they are only used to achieve the handover criteria of existing local market companies.

Market-Launch-Pipeline: Die MLP describes the number and size of new markets which are currently in the management process *company2newmarket*. Based on this information, companies can assess their growth potential in new international markets.

Market penetration strategy: This is a market expansion policy that is characterized by parallel entry into several individual markets.

Market preparation: This is the second step of the management process *company2newmarket*. The goal of this step is to design and to test a business and process model for the markets selected in step one.

Market seekers: Companies that search for new clients in new international markets to whom they can sell their products.

Market timing strategies: This is a competitive strategy which helps to determine the right time for market entry, for example as a first mover or a late follower. Each market timing strategy requires different behaviour and a different market approach.

MENA: Abbreviation for a group of countries and regions – in this case the Middle East and North Africa – with similar characteristics.

MNE: Abbreviation for a multi-national enterprise.

N

New entrants: A new entrant is a company which is currently entering a new market. It depends on the market structure and size whether existing competitors will react or not.

Next11: describes a group of emerging growth markets following on from the BRIC countries

NGO / NPO: Today, non-governmental and non-profit-making organizations are very important stakeholders for MNEs.

O

Outsourcing: Transfer of activities to another company in one's own country or in a foreign market.

Off-shoring: Transfer of activities to another foreign country.

P

Phase model of market entry: In general, companies use a low-risk market entry form in the "market entry" step but due to experience and knowhow they might choose a riskier market growth form in the "market development and growth" step.

Polycentrism: This describes an international company with a host country orientation and a preference for choosing personnel from the host country to fill all the positions in the subsidiary as well as systems and ways of managing and operating that are customary in the host country.

R

Real-Option-Theory: The ROT is a method for calculating the value of a real growth option in a new international market. The value of this option is added to the value of the local market company.

Regiocentrism: Description of an international company with a regional orientation. A region can be defined as a number of countries from the same geographical region which have a similar culture. Often it is identical with a free trade area such as the European Union, NAFTA, GCC, or Mercosur.

Reputation management: This is a strategy which needs to be implemented in all areas and aspects of a company to create trust, reliability and credibility among stakeholders.

Resource seekers: Companies that search for new (natural, financial, and human) resources in new international markets.

S

Self-reference criterion: The unconscious reference to one's own cultural values in comparison to other cultures.

Shotgun clause: This is a dispute resolution clause in joint venture contracts. In case of disputes, one joint venture partner can name a price to buy out his partner. Once the other partner has received the price, he can buy out the joint venture partner for the same price. This is to provide fair pricing.

Skimming: This is a pricing strategy in new international markets. First, the price of the base product is high to attract opinion leaders and to maximize profits. Second, with growing competition and increasing product differentiation prices are gradually lowered to remain competitive and to defend market share and at the same time increase market entry barriers for new entrants.

SPOT: When a company designs a business or process model for an international market, it should start with a definition of its strategy. On the basis of this, the processes and the organization to implement the strategy are developed. Finally, the information and communication system are added to allow efficient communication within the organization.

Step: The management process *company2newmarket* consists of four steps: market evaluation and selection, market preparation, market entry, and market development and growth.

Supranational forms of collaboration between states: In general, states work together on a global, regional, and bilateral level. Apart from bilateral talks and agreements, supranational special purpose organizations like the UN or the WTO are used to organize international collaboration.

T

Task: Each step of the management process *company2newmarket* consists of several tasks which need to be completed to reach the objective of the step in question.

Timing Strategies: The timing of the market entry has a huge influence on market success. There are different strategies available from first mover to late follower.

Tool: Tools are used to implement the tasks which are defined for each step of the management process *company2newmarket*. This leads to higher quality, which means in detail greater reliability, comparability, and efficiency of results in different international markets.

Trading blocs (regional): Groups of nations that integrate economic and political activities (free-trade areas).

Transnational organization structure: A MNE with a diversified product portfolio use this organisation structure to take advantage of global opportunities.

TRIADE: North America, Japan, and the European Union form the so-called TRIADE of industrialized and highly developed countries and regions.

Bibliography and Further Reading

The following bibliography is a small selection of valuable sources on international and intercultural management. It provides global managers with books and tips on international organizations to help them to carry out their every day work more quickly and efficiently. It also includes a number of regional (e.g. free trade areas), national, state and private providers such as, for Germany, the Chambers of Foreign Trade (www.ahk.de) or Societies for Promoting Exports (www.gtai.de), whose links I will be pleased to send upon request.

Dülfer, E. / Jöstingmeier, B. (2008): Internationales Management in unterschiedlichen Kulturbereichen, Oldenbourg Wissenschaftsverlag (International Management in Diverse Cultures)

GRE (= Global Reporting Initiative): https://www.globalreporting.org/Pages/default.aspx (publishes standards for sustainability reports)

Hall, E. T. (1976): Beyond Culture, Anchor Books

Hofstede, G. / Hofstede, G. J. / Minkov, M. (2010): Cultures and Organizations – Software of the Mind: Intercultural Cooperation and Its Importance for Survival, 3rd edition, McGraw Hill Professional

Hofstede, G.: http://geert-hofstede.com/national-culture.html (publishes his research about national cultures)

ICC (= International Chamber of Commerce): http://www.iccwbo.org (publishes trade tools, research like for example the famous INCOTERMS and helps with dispute settlement)

ILO (= international labour organisation): www.ilo.org (publishes for example Global Employment and Wage Reports, the international Labour Standards together with a rich database)

IMD Business School: http://www.imd.org/wcc/ (publishes the World Competitiveness Yearbook)

IMF (= International Monetary Fund): http://www.imf.org/external/data.htm (publishes current and reliable economic data about all member states)

ITC (= a joint organization of the UNCTAD and WTO with the (one) goal to improve the ability of small- and medium-sized enterprises (SMEs) to integrate into the world trading system) manages the website www.trademap.org and www.intracen.org with trade statistics for international business development

Neubert, Michael / B. Bauhofer (2012): Wie gut ist mein Ruf? (How Good is my Reputation?), Gabal Verlag

Neubert, Michael (2011): Internationale Markterschließung (Developing International Markets), 3rd edition, mi-Wirtschaftsbuch – Münchner Verlagsgruppe

OECD (Organisation for Economic Co-Operation and Development): www.oecd. org (publishes a lot of interesting information for its member states with a view to increasing global economic cooperation)

Porter, M. E. (2004): Competitive Strategy: Techniques for Analysing Industries and Competitors, Free Press

Porter, M. E. (1998): The Competitive Advantage of Nations, Free Press

Root, F. R. (1994): Entry Strategies for International Markets, Jossey-Bass Books

Simon, H. (2012): Hidden Champions – Aufbruch nach Globalia: Die Erfolgsstrategien unbekannter Weltmarktführer, Campus Verlag (Hidden Champions – Heading for a Global World: The Successful Strategies of Unknown Global Market Leaders), Campus Verlag

Transparency: http://transparency.org/whatwedo/pub/corruption_perceptions_index_2012 (publishes the global corruption perception index)

Trompenaars, F. / Hampden-Turner, C. (2012): Riding the Waves of Culture: Understanding Cultural Diversity in Business, 3rd edition, Nicholas Brealey Publishing

UNESCO: http://unstats.un.org/unsd/demographic/sconcerns/education/ (publishes the demographic yearbook with information about education and qualification in all member states)

UN Global Compact: http://www.unglobalcompact.org/AboutTheGC/TheTen Principles/index.html (is famous for its ten principles)

WEF (world economic forum): http://www.weforum.org (publishes a huge variety of reports about the global economy, regions and countries)

WIPO (= World Intellectual Property Organisation): http://www.wipo.int/portal/index.html.en (is the global IP reference source)

World Bank: http://info.worldbank.org/governance/wgi/ (worldwide governance indicators)

World Fact Book published by the Central Intelligence Agency (USA): https://www.cia.gov/library/publications/the-world-factbook/ (valuable source of current and reliable information about every country)

WTO (= World Trade Organisation): http://www.wto.org/english/tratop_e/region_e/region_e.htm (publishes all global free trade agreements and a great deal of additional information on global trade)

WVS (= World Value Survey): http://www.worldvaluessurvey.org (carries out surveys to learn more about values and cultural changes in societies all over the world.

Index

How to get your free e-book:

1. Go to *www.campus.de/ebookinside*

2. Enter your personal **download code** and fill out the form

3. Choose your preferred file **format** (EPUB or PDF)

4. Click the button at the end of the form and you will receive an email with your personal **download link**

YOUR PERSONAL DOWNLOAD CODE:

TEX2U-DWLXU-SMR7P